USING
REALITY THERAPY

USING
REALITY THERAPY

Robert E. Wubbolding

Foreword by William Glasser, M.D.

Harper & Row, Publishers, New York
Grand Rapids, Philadelphia, St. Louis, San Francisco
London, Singapore, Sydney, Tokyo, Toronto

Chapter 10 is an expansion of an article originally published in the *Journal of Reality Therapy,* 1981, I, 1, pp. 4–7.

Figure 1 is adapted from William Glasser, *Basic Concepts of Reality Therapy,* copyright © 1986 by Robert E. Wubbolding.

Figure 4 is reproduced by permission of William Glasser.

Copyeditor: Carole Berglie
Designer: Erich Hobbing
Index by Maro Riofrancos

Library of Congress Cataloging-in-Publication Data

Wubbolding, Robert E.
  Using reality therapy.

  Includes index.
  1. Reality therapy.   I. Title.
RC489.R37W83   1988   616.89'14   87-46183
ISBN 0-06-055123-2   88 89 90 91 92 FG 10 9 8 7 6 5 4 3 2 1
ISBN 0-06-096266-6 (pbk.)   93 94 95 96 97 RRD   10 9 8 7 6

To Sandie,
the most need-fulfilling person
in my life

Contents

Foreword by William Glasser, M.D.   vii

Preface   ix

Acknowledgments   x

1. The Mind and How It Works   1

2. Reality Therapy in Action: Guidelines for a Counseling Relationship   10

3. What to Avoid in a Counseling Relationship   22

4. Procedures: Exploring the "Picture Album" (Wants), Needs, and Perceptions   28

5. Procedures: Exploring Total Behavior and Evaluating   39

6. Procedures: Planning and Commitment   58

7. Using Paradoxical Techniques   74

8. Marriage and Family Counseling   91

9. Two Cases: A Single Woman and a Married Couple   110

10. The Replacement Program: Reality Therapy and Personal Growth   122

11. Applications to the World of Work   142

Contents

12. Questioning and Questions   161
     Postscript   172
     Appendix   173
     Bibliography   174
     Index   177

Foreword

by William Glasser, M.D.

These pages contain ideas crucial to the effective practice of Reality Therapy. When I first developed the principles of Reality Therapy I attempted to present to practitioners a no-nonsense method of helping people that could be used by counselors, therapists, teachers, parents, and others. Subsequent to that I utilized the principles of Control Theory as the basis for the practice of Reality Therapy. This theory of brain functioning, as I have extended it, provides a comprehensive explanation of how we behave. In other words, everything we do, think, feel, even our physiologic behaviors and most especially the interplay among these elements, can be understood in the light of Control Theory.

Robert E. Wubbolding has integrated Control Theory and the practice of Reality Therapy and has made the result understandable and eminently useful to the reader. He breaks new ground by initiating a Reality Therapy model for marriage and family counseling. He has also integrated paradoxical techniques into the practice of Reality Therapy while explaining in the context of Control Theory why they can be effective.

Wubbolding's ideas about why the practice of Reality Therapy involves skillful questioning adds a new dimension to the understanding of theory and practice. His jargon-free writing is the result of many year's experience and study. In my close association with him I have watched him extend the ideas of Reality

Therapy by making the Mental Picture Album a concept that can be used in Counseling.

Wubbolding adds positive behaviors to the basic concept of Reality Therapy showing that effective behavior is developmental rather than static. His thinking is as subtle as it is practical. Moreover, the activities he suggests will help the reader apply the ideas in personal as well as professional ways. If you follow the suggestions for this personal application you will be on the road to more effectively controlled living.

Finally, it should be noted that I have repeatedly referred to Bob as "one of my closest associates." This book illustrates why I say this again. I recommend his writings to all people seeking a fuller understanding of how to improve their own personal and professional lives.

Preface

This book is an attempt to illustrate how Reality Therapy can be used in a practical, methodical, down-to-earth way. It contains usable suggestions on how to talk to persons in need of help. These suggestions are seen in the context of the well-grounded theory of brain functioning called Control Theory. A cookbook or simplistic "how to" approach has been shunned here. The ideas are to be integrated into the practitioner's personality and style of communication.

Moreover, in any written description of the art of counseling, one very important element cannot be adequately presented—*Timing*. The appropriate timing of counseling interventions depends on two main factors: the ability of the therapist to cue into the nonverbal messages of the client, and the finely honed instincts of the therapist, which are developed only with practice and reflective evaluation of one's own therapeutic performance. Nonetheless, an attempt has been made to describe specific ways to establish a healthful environment for counseling as well as specific procedures that lead to the growth and self-fulfillment of clients.

Another purpose of this book is to extend the scope of Reality Therapy to marriage counseling, use of paradoxical techniques, supervision, and self-help. Reality Therapy, therefore, is not seen as a narrow, doctrinaire theory or a set of prescriptions. Rather, it is a philosophy of life which requires extensive application to nearly every aspect of human relationships.

Acknowledgments

Gratitude is especially due to Dr. William Glasser, whose life work is the inspiration for this book. His contribution to the helping professions and therefore to the public is immeasurable. I especially appreciate his genius, his total acceptance of the people around him, his quick-wittedness, and the challenge he provides to those who call him teacher. Naomi Glasser also deserves a special thanks. Both have provided many suggestions for refining the ideas contained in this book. *Ad multos annos.*

My clients as well as the thousands of persons who have attended my classes and workshops deserve recognition. With their help the ideas in this book have been tested, challenged, and refined. My colleagues and fellow Reality Therapists deserve a special thanks for being such good listeners.

My brothers and sisters, nieces and nephews share in the influence that this book might enjoy. Each in his or her own way has contributed.

My energetic secretaries, Ceil Schoen and Ruby Wardlaw, have shown heroic patience, understanding, and support during the long hours of preparation of this book. Kathy Riga is thanked for her accurate and prompt work at the computer.

Finally, I wish to thank my wife, Sandie, who provided encouragement in times of doubt, excitement in times of success, and honesty at all times. Her support, prodding, and affection continue to fulfill my "wants and needs."

* 1 *

The Mind
and How It Works

In vaudevillian comedy there was a classic joke. Question: "Why did the chicken cross the road?" Answer: "To get to the other side!" This ancient question and answer represents a profound truth: that behavior exhibited by a living creature has a purpose. It is not aimless, but is designed to accomplish something. In human beings, behavior is designed to accomplish the fulfillment of human needs and wants.

The theory and method utilized in Reality Therapy is based, therefore, on the notion that human behavior is purposeful and originates from within rather than from external stimuli. William Glasser (1980) stated that the most fundamental needs which drive human beings are fourfold.

Belonging, or Love

The need to belong and to be involved with people is a force that drives all human beings, especially in what Glasser (1972) has labeled an "identity society" in which there is emphasis on the importance of personal relationships. In an age in which there is an abundance of social clubs, self-help groups, meetings, mixers, singles' bars, church gatherings, and the like, it is evident that the need to belong, to overcome loneliness is an ubiquitous force in

1

our society. W. C. Fields once said: "The only cure for insomnia is to get more sleep." Likewise, the cure for loneliness, an ailment of the identity society, is involvement with people.

In my counseling and teaching, I have divided the need to belong into three forms—social belonging, work belonging, and family belonging—for the fulfillment of the need takes place in several settings. It is useful to ask how a client is fulfilling his or her need in those settings: with friends, on the job (if employed), and with family or relatives.

Power (Achievement, Self-Worth, Recognition)

The need for power is often expressed through competition with people around us. It is also expressed in achieving something; for example, swimming or jogging noncompetitively can also provide a sense of achievement or self-worth. Making plans and following through on them can help fulfill the need for power.

When I think of power I'm instantly reminded of Mother Theresa, that marvelous woman who has shunned the worldly status and leadership which help many others to fulfill their power needs. Yet her influence in serving the poor of Calcutta has placed her among the genuinely powerful of the world.

Fun

Aristotle defined a human being as a creature who is risible—that is, who can laugh. Other Greek philosophers described one of the attributes as "*eutropelia*," or the virtue of having fun. It is also a fact that children learn through play. So important is play, according to Glasser (1985), that it would be virtually impossible for children to learn without it. The need for fun, of course, continues into adulthood. It is a force that expresses itself in every human endeavor.

Freedom

The final need which drives human beings is the urge to make choices, to move from place to place and to be internally free. The

2

bonds of slavery are not merely external. Frankl (1963) points out that in World War II he retained his inner freedom even though he was in Auschwitz for several years. He was still able to choose how he would respond to the horrible events he experienced and witnessed. Although relatively few people must rely on such elemental choices to express freedom, still the need for freedom can be hindered by a lack of impulse control, by drugs, by psychoses, as well as by external restraints. So fundamental is the drive for freedom that people will die for it. This is abundantly clear from the study of history, and this paradox serves to illustrate how deeply rooted and pervasive is the need for freedom.

Such needs are present in all human beings. Glasser has repeatedly stated in his lectures that these needs are "genetic instructions." We are born with the instructions and all human beings possess them. Yet these human needs are fulfilled in very specific ways. We all exist in a dimension called "time." We must fulfill the needs from moment to moment, and so each person develops an inner "picture album" of specific wants. This "picture album" contains precise images of how we wish to fulfill those needs. For example, though we all have a need for belonging, fulfilling that need by joining the local Kiwanis Club is a picture in the minds of only those who belong to that particular club. Power is a need common to all human beings, too. Some fulfill it through the specific want, or picture, of exercising, or of engaging in politics, of saving money, or of spending money! The need is common to all persons, but the want is specific and unique for each person.

The same can be said of the needs for fun and freedom. Skydiving is seen as desirable by some people. It fulfills needs for fun and freedom. Yet others testify that it is completely undesirable and that they would never insert it in their "picture albums." And so the first principle underlying Reality Therapy can be stated as follows:

PRINCIPLE 1:   HUMAN BEINGS ARE MOTIVATED TO FULFILL NEEDS AND WANTS. HUMAN NEEDS ARE COMMON TO ALL PEOPLE. WANTS ARE UNIQUE TO EACH INDIVIDUAL.

3

When human beings get what they want, they are satisfied. A state of rest is achieved. When there is a gap or difference (frustration) between what they want and what they perceive they are getting, they are moved to execute some behavior. Thus, as a reader of this book you read on because you want to know what comes later in the text. Since the later material is not yet perceived by you as already known, you continue reading. There are always discrepancies (frustrations) between what we want and what we perceive we are getting. This is why we continue to produce behaviors (such as reading, turning pages, and so on). And so another principle underlying Reality Therapy is as follows:

PRINCIPLE 2: THE DIFFERENCE (FRUSTRATION) BE-TWEEN WHAT HUMAN BEINGS WANT AND WHAT THEY PERCEIVE THEY ARE GETTING FROM THEIR ENVIRON-MENT PRODUCES SPECIFIC BEHAVIORS.

Total behavior comprises the elements of Doing, Thinking, Feeling, and Physiology. Though these behaviors are not really separable, they are distinguished here because often one or the other is more prominent. Thus when human beings do not have what they want, they attempt to get it by total behavior (Doing, Thinking, Feeling, and Physiologic Behavior). We attempt to mold the world as a sculptor molds clay—to match internal pictures. When Michelangelo chiseled marble, he could see the unfinished figure in the stone. We are all sculptors in our behavior, attempting to change the world outside us to match our internal pictures of what we want. This is true of the most simple as well as the most complex behaviors. For example, we want a feeling of comfort. When we have an itch, we feel slight discomfort. The gap between the want for comfort and the perception of discomfort drives us to move our hand to the itch and scratch it! Equally, in a more complex situation, a parent wants a child to study and to excel in school. The child refuses to study, and the parent nags, and nags, and nags, often knowing that nagging will not get the desired result. This and many other Doing behaviors are very ineffective in fulfilling wants.

Besides these Doing behaviors, there are also Feeling behaviors—that is, behaviors in which feeling is more prominent. We generate positive and negative feelings to get what we want. We want to feel positive, so we generate positive thoughts, looking for the bright side of life, or we take action to feel better. Conversely, a person generates angering or depressing behaviors to close the gaps (frustrations). Even angering, depressing, guilting, and all the other negative Feeling behaviors are an attempt to get what we want. Thus when a person generates guilt after making a fool of himself at a party, the guilt is an attempt to change what happened, to make it go away. Perhaps the person wants to see himself as a kind, considerate individual and wishes others to see the same qualities. But being rude at a party created a large gap between these two pictures, and the guilt is an attempt to close that gap. Does it work? You, the reader, can decide.

Sometimes the Thinking aspect of total behavior stands out. Planning, self-praise, self-criticism, evaluation of our own or others' behaviors, and many other kinds of self-talk constitute the Thinking system. Ironically, even though the Doing behavior is stressed in Reality Therapy, the first point of entry for changing behavior is through the Thinking aspect. In the practice of Reality Therapy discussed in Chapter 5, clients make judgments on the Doing aspect of behavior by asking the question, "Is what you're doing helping you?" Now, the third principle underlying Reality Therapy can be defined:

PRINCIPLE 3: HUMAN BEHAVIOR—COMPOSED OF DOING, THINKING, FEELING, AND PHYSIOLOGIC BEHAVIORS—IS PURPOSEFUL; THAT IS, IT IS DESIGNED TO CLOSE THE GAP BETWEEN WHAT THE PERSON WANTS AND WHAT THE PERSON PERCEIVES HE OR SHE IS GETTING.

Finally, it cannot be emphasized too strongly that behaviors come from inside and that most of them are choices. (Psychosomatic ailments and psychoses are not choices.) Reality Therapy rests on the notion that we choose our fate. We are the captain of our ship and we can control it. The fact that behaviors are generated is emphasized in this book and in the literature on Reality

Therapy by the use of verbs and *ing* words. Thus an angry person is said to be "angering" rather than to "be angry." Clients are encouraged to say, "Today I am guilting" or, "Last night I was depressing." Phrases like "fit of depression," "anxiety attack," or "stressful job" are meaningless. Thus the fourth principle is enunciated:

PRINCIPLE 4: DOING, THINKING, AND FEELING ARE IN-SEPARABLE ASPECTS OF BEHAVIOR AND ARE GENER-ATED FROM WITHIN. MOST OF THEM ARE CHOICES.

Throughout this book behaviors are described as action words— verbs. Reality Therapists do not see depression, anxiety, joy, hope, and the like as static conditions. Since these behaviors are generated, they are referred to with *ing* endings; thus, "depress-ing," "anxieting," "psychosing," "joying," "self-confidencing," and so on.

When we seek to mold our world to get what we want, it is obvious that the desired material object itself does not enter our inner world. A perception is the more precise object of the desire. Human beings desire to see themselves as adequate, as compe-tent, as belonging to someone, as being athletic, as being without worries, and so on. These perceptions are filtered from the exter-nal world and incorporated into part of our inner world. It is helpful to see perceptions as on either a high or low level. To view the environment from a low level of perception is to be able to withhold judgment, to accept it without approving or disap-proving. One of the basic principles underlying all counseling is that the counselor be able to withhold judgment about the client. An effective therapist can talk nonjudgmentally to most clients who might exhibit behaviors far different from those of the coun-selor. On the other hand, to view the world from a high level of perception is to make judgments about it, to put values on issues or events, to "take a stand" either mentally or by words and actions. And so, the final principle is as follows:

PRINCIPLE 5: HUMAN BEINGS SEE THE WORLD THROUGH PERCEPTIONS. THERE ARE TWO GENERAL

LEVELS OF PERCEPTION: LOW AND HIGH. THE LOW
LEVEL OF PERCEPTION IMPLIES KNOWLEDGE OF EVENTS
OR SITUATIONS. A HIGH LEVEL OF PERCEPTION GIVES
VALUES TO THOSE EVENTS OR SITUATIONS.

The preceding discussion is not intended to be an exhaustive
treatment of the principles underlying Reality Therapy. The goal
here is to present briefly and simply the main principles of the
theory as they relate to counseling. For a more detailed description, consult the works of Powers (1973) and Glasser (1985).

Exercises

Described below are several incidents. They are events that happen from time to time and are presented here to help you view
the world within the framework of the principles just given. Try
to answer the questions using the concepts described earlier.

Incident 1

You return to your car to discover that it has four flat tires. You
become so upset you kick the car, scream, and begin to cry. You
then look around you, and you see that you are parked in front of
a tire store. You notice a salesperson coming out to talk to you.
He has a helpful look on his face. Why are you upset and why is
he apparently happy?

Incident 2

Your employee spends a lot of time loafing, complaining about
his job, saying the boss is unfair. You talk to this well-
intentioned employee and help him do better, work harder, and
so on. He later returns to you and remarks how the other workers
have changed. Even the boss is better than he used to be. Explain
how and why this happened.

Incident 3

A young man moves into the dorm of a small college as a freshman. He hates the school. The rules are strict, and he breaks most of them and flunks his first semester. He then decides to throw himself into the program, keep the rules, and study hard. At the end of the year he discovers that he likes the school and returns for another year. Explain this using the principles described above.

Incident 4

A woman is nervous about taking a driver's exam. She tries to overcome the nervousing behavior by practicing and studying. The more she tries to overcome it, the more she generates feelings of nervousness. She then tries just the opposite: to feel nervousness for ten minutes a day imagining that she has made a fool of herself during the driver's test. She reports that, "the more I tried to feel nervous, the less nervous I felt." Why?

Incident 5

John loves Mary. His theme song is "Can't live if livin' is without you." Mary meets another man and tells John good-bye. John feels very depressed for months. He then meets Carol and gradually starts to develop a relationship with her. He feels better. Explain this incident and how would you change the words to the song for him.

A Further Word About the Mind

The history of theories which have attempted to explain the working of the brain reveals that theorists have always relied upon current technology. In the nineteenth century, theorists saw the brain as a steam engine that drives the mechanism of the human body. In the early twentieth century, the brain was viewed as an intricate information exchange similar to a miniature but infinitely more complex telephone switchboard. Since the 1940s, the computer has served as a model for several theories. One such theory sees the brain as a cybernetic servomechanism, or control system. A similar theory views the brain as two computers, right and left. A third approach, based on laser technology, explains the brain as a hologram containing images of the external world.

The theory that best explains how we live our lives on a daily basis sees the brain as a "control system" which seeks to control, maneuver, or mold the external world to satisfy an internal purpose.

Control theorists have investigated the functioning of the brain for many years. Most recently, Glasser has brought the theory to a clinical level, extending it to new, practical applications. The principles described in this chapter are based on the viewpoint that the brain is a "control system." For a detailed explanation, consult *Control Theory* (Glasser 1984).

* 2 *

Reality Therapy in Action: Guidelines for a Counseling Relationship

The process of Reality Therapy consists of two major ingredients: setting an environment conducive to change and utilizing various procedures leading to change. Formerly these elements were known as the Eight Steps of Reality Therapy (Glasser 1980), but they have been reconceptualized to emphasize that Reality Therapy is not a simplistic, lockstep method to be followed blindly (Glasser 1986).

These elements can be described most efficiently as a Cycle of Counseling Using Reality Therapy, as shown in Figure 1. The cycle illustrates that there is an overall sequence to the implementation of the theory of Reality Therapy, that the environment is the foundation upon which rests the procedures, and that there are specific guidelines (dos and don'ts) for building a relationship with the client. Moreover, the relationship between the former Eight Steps, as described in previous writings, and the current process of Reality Therapy is clarified.

BE FRIENDS

The practice of Reality Therapy begins with an effort to establish an authentic, warm, and caring relationship. In our society, relationships are of paramount importance. Glasser (1971), Wrenn (1973), Ford (1977), and many others have testified that we live in a society in which personal involvement with each other is highly regarded. Counselors and therapists are not alone in their recognition of this fact. In conversations with teachers, speech therapists, reading specialists, and many others, I have learned that the relationship between helper and client is crucial. People enjoy and tend to buy more from a salesperson who genuinely cares about the customer. How many people return to a store, a bank, or a shop because of the personal involvement shown by the owner or clerk? The age-old phrase, "the customer is always right" is based not only on profit, but on personal relationship. Peters (1982, 1986) makes this abundantly clear in his recent writings. Many people have a special appreciation for their family physician's bedside manner. Similarly, I once asked a tour guide in Europe, "What makes a good tour from your point of view?" He replied, "If I can get the people to trust me, we can have more fun and they will do more things than they would have done. . . ." His comment summed up much that is true in counseling, especially in Reality Therapy. As I'll describe soon, clients are helped to make plans. They will do this only if there is involvement, friendship, and a feeling of trust. The work of Carkhuff and Truax (1979) substantiates the fact that positive regard is essential for effective counseling and psychotherapy.

Use Attending Behaviors

There are many models of attending behaviors. Especially useful in the practice of Reality Therapy are those described by Ivey (1980): eye contact and facial expression—looking at the client without staring, and displaying a genuine interest; physical posture—sitting in an open, receptive position; verbal following—tracking the client's comments and reflecting in a manner that communicates listening behaviors by the counselor; nonverbal behavior—attending to the client's manner of expression, such as tone of voice; paraphrasing—restating the client's comments occasionally. In Reality Therapy, these skills serve as a foundation for an enhanced relationship between counselor and client.

11

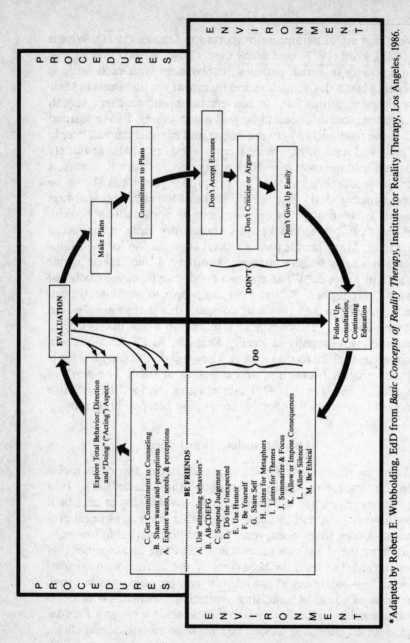

ENVIRONMENT

Commitment to Plans

Make Plans

Don't Accept Excuses

Don't Criticize or Argue

Don't Give Up Easily

EVALUATION

DON'T

Follow Up, Consultation, Continuing Education

Explore Total Behavior: Direction and "Doing" ("Acting") Aspect

DO

-------- **BE FRIENDS** --------

A. Use "attending behaviors"
B. AB-CDEFG
C. Suspend Judgement
D. Do the Unexpected
E. Use Humor
F. Be Yourself
G. Share Self
H. Listen for Metaphors
I. Listen for Themes
J. Summarize & Focus
K. Allow or Impose Consequences
L. Allow Silence
M. Be Ethical

C. Get Commitment to Counseling
B. Share wants and perceptions
A. Explore wants, needs, & perceptions

PROCEDURES

ENVIRONMENT

*Adapted by Robert E. Wubbolding, EdD from *Basic Concepts of Reality Therapy*, Institute for Reality Therapy, Los Angeles, 1986.

FIGURE 1: CYCLE OF COUNSELING USING REALITY THERAPY

Practice the ABs

In my teaching of Reality Therapy, I have attempted to summarize several guidelines for establishing an ongoing friendship with clients. Among them are the ABs (AB = "always be").

Always Be Courteous. Even if the client is angry, abusive, and upset, the counselor should be kind and courteous, attempting to remain calm and unintimidated. A warm statement such as, "Would you like to sit down and discuss it with me?" or, "I can help you if you will talk to me about it" is often very useful. Establishing the friendship on the counselor's terms is important. These "terms" are expressed not by using one's own anger, but by behaving in ways characterized by strength and flexibility rather than by weakness and rigidity. Most of the time, of course, the client is not angry with the counselor. It is important for the counselor to allow clients to have their angry feelings, recognizing that angering is the best possible choice at a given moment —in the client's view of things. In other words, the Reality Therapist attempts to look at the client's angering behavior from a low level of perception. Looking at the angering in a rational way or even from a level at which judgment is suspended momentarily is not easy, yet it is helpful for the counselor to exhibit Doing behaviors that parallel a low level of perception when a client is upset.

Always Be Determined. Reality Therapy is based on the principle that total behaviors are almost always chosen. And so, more efficient and more helpful behaviors are available to most clients who have problems. An attitude that is helpful, then, is to decide, with deep conviction, that there is a better way to live, accomplished through generating more effective behaviors. In teaching Reality Therapy to teachers, Glasser is fond of saying that a message to be communicated to students is that, "this is a 'work-it-out' classroom." Working it out is, as he says, "the way it is." This is idealistic, of course, and ideals are not met 100 percent of the time by 100 percent of those reaching for them, but it is a positive and powerful belief, crucial to a genuine relationship. A seriously depressing woman once told me in the beginning of her second session, "You just *assumed* that my depression would be temporary." Borrowing a phrase from another therapist I responded, "The thought never occurred to me that it could be permanent."

Always Be Enthusiastic. The motto for an enthusiastic Reality Therapist is, "If I'm down, get up. If I'm up, stay up." The application of the behavior-is-chosen principle to one's own self is relevant here. Even when the therapist is less than enthusiastic, he or she needs to make a decision to be in *at least* a minimally pleasant mood, preferably in a positive mood when talking to clients. Thus an effective counselor engages in need- and want-fulfilling behaviors outside of counseling. Ongoing, painful, and serious frustration suffered by the therapist will influence the effectiveness of counseling in addition to diminishing the strength of the counselor.

Always Be Firm. Persons practicing Reality Therapy function in many settings: schools, employment agencies, hospitals, correctional facilities, private practice, counseling offices, and so on. Generally there are rules, and they are often enforced by counselors. Assuming these rules are reasonable, they should be administered without apology, much as a police officer writes a traffic ticket in a friendly, calm, and nondefensive manner. But this firmness is also characteristic of the effective application of Reality Therapy guidelines and procedures. Clear value judgments are asked for, often insisted on, by the therapist. Definite and firm plans are formulated, and no excuses are tolerated. Such firmness is in no way in contradiction to empathy, kindness, or openness to the client and his or her hurts. These are part of the first component, "Always Be Courteous."

Always Be Genuine. Being honest and straightforward with clients is crucial. The effective Reality Therapist teaches in an implicit way by personal example. The client learns that mental health and a better life are enhanced when human relationships

14

are based on openness and directness rather than on avoidance and manipulation.

Suspend Judgment

If a counselor is to maintain professional relationships, suspending judgment is crucial. This implies that he or she is able to see clients' behaviors from a low level of perception—that is, without judging or condemning. This does not imply agreement with destructive behaviors. It simply means that the therapist is able initially to view clients' behaviors as their best efforts to fulfill their needs. The converse of this guideline is to view clients' behaviors from a high level of perception—that is, to put a value (approval or disapproval) on clients' best efforts.

Do the Unexpected

A helpful guideline in establishing a friendly environment is occasionally (but not exclusively) to respond in an unexpected way (see Chapter 7). For example, the client expects the therapist to discuss failure behaviors such as drugs, past problems, and the like. Unexpectedly, the counselor discusses successful positive behaviors. Instead of asking, "Why do you take drugs?" the counselor asks, "When was the last time you had fun without getting into trouble and without taking drugs?" In family counseling, there is a tendency to focus on one member who is the "identified patient." It is often helpful to spend a session in which the therapist focuses on everyone *except* the identified patient. As stated in Chapter 1, the purpose of all behavior is to control or mold the external world. When counselors focus on behaviors other than the obvious ones, they are attempting to remove the payoff for manipulative and destructive behaviors. Thus, for one person to effectively control another person, the latter must be controllable.

For instance, one way to avoid an argument is to agree. This is especially useful when talking with the "argument lover." To simply say, "You're probably right" removes the payoff for the person wishing to argue. I once met an overly eager salesperson who respectfully sought to entrap me in an argument by asking why I didn't want the product. My answer was, "Simply because I don't want it." He repeated the question hoping I would argue, thereby giving him the opportunity to demolish my arguments and make a sale. This time my answer was, "Simply because." The third attempt on his part resulted only in a shrug of the shoulders on my part. At this point my would-be arguer left for greener pastures. Dreikurs (1972) uses the phrase, "Take the sail out of their wind." If the counselor drops the sail, there is nothing to blow against, and the wind dissipates. Frequently, people seek counseling because they suffer painful frustrations. By doing the unexpected the therapist helps clients look at other inner wants and set aside the pain temporarily. To deal with problems and diminish pain, it is often helpful to set the problem aside for a while rather than "deal with it" directly (see Chapters 5 and 7).

Use Humor

Introducing humor to the counseling session is crucial, especially when the problems are serious. The humor should be good-natured, not hostile; democratic, not patronizing; and genuine, not forced. Humor should be well timed and point out some human foible or incongruity. It should help both client and counselor laugh and learn. Obviously there are situations in which it is counterproductive—for example, when the client is generating feelings of grief at a recent death of a loved one.

In general, the therapist teaches the client that, through a sense of humor, "life can be beautiful," there is hope, and "laughter is the best medicine."

Be Yourself

The practice of Reality Therapy appears to be structured and precise, and in many ways it is. Yet it should be adapted to the therapist's own personality. It can be used by the talkative or reticent therapist, by the person who is emotionally expressive or one who is more reserved. Though there are structure and precision, still the theory and practice should be seen more as a loose-fitting overcoat than as a tailor-made wet suit!

Share Yourself

The Cycle of Counseling should not be viewed as merely a technique to be followed mechanically. The first step is, "Be Friends." To be a friend, a person must share him- or herself and be in some way vulnerable to the other person. Aristotle stated that part of friendship included an *exchange* among people. It is important that the therapist be willing to share him- or herself. The counseling friendship has reached a higher level when the client begins to ask the therapist a few questions about his or her own life.

Like any element in the cycle, sharing one's self can be overdone. It is not an expression of neurotic behavior, but a healthy, spontaneous, genuine, noningratiating willingness to allow the client to enter the world of the therapist.

Listen for Metaphors

Clients frequently use figures of speech to describe their perceptions of themselves, of others, or of their situations. "I feel like a door mat." "My husband acts like a lamb sometimes and a lion at other times." "I draw a chalk line around myself and I don't let anyone inside."

Metaphors can come spontaneously from clients, or they can be suggested by the counselor. "Where would you place yourself on a continuum—floor mat at one end and bulldozer at the other?" "It seems you carry a monkey on your back. Would you like to leave it here when you go home today?" "When it comes to the energy you expend in the relationship, or on the job, or in school, do you see yourself as having a .250 batting average, a .330, or a .400? Do you want to raise it?" Witmer (1985) describes three purposes to such figures of speech: "to give us greater understanding of what is already known, to provide us with greater insight into the unknown, and to enable us to express that which has aesthetic and emotional intensity." In the context of Reality Therapy, these purposes serve to establish an environment conducive to change. Of themselves, they do not immediately constitute procedures that bring about change.

Listen for Themes

Frequently, clients describe their situations in terms of themes. The Reality Therapist listens for, clarifies, and reflects back the clients' themes. It should be noted that themes to be emphasized by the counselor are those related to Reality Therapy, especially the procedures described below. The therapist might discover the theme of depression or, more specifically, that the client gets depressed on weekends. In group counseling, the therapist can effectively establish a trusting atmosphere by tying together the wants or perceptions of the group. Themes are brought into the open by such statements as, "Each member of the group seems to want to have more control in his or her life, either at home or at work." Though the search for themes is not unique to Reality Therapy, nevertheless in this method it is foundational; that is, it is a way to establish an environment upon which are built the procedures that follow.

Use Summaries and Focus

This type of human interaction is part of many counseling methods. In Reality Therapy, it is used in a unique manner. Instead of paraphrasing everything stated by the client, the effective Reality Therapist focuses on themes. A summary might be limited only to the wants of the client, for example. In talking with an angry, unwilling teenage client, I summarized ten minutes of vitriolic complaints by saying, "You want your parents off your back, you want to keep your own hours, you want them to feed and water you, you want to be left alone, and you don't want me to try to help you!" Other summaries might be limited to strength-building behaviors—that is, behaviors that resulted in effective control, behaviors that helped, behaviors that did not work, or value judgments about what might work in the future. In other words, in Reality Therapy summaries are specifically related to the Cycle of Counseling and to the theory underlying it, and they can take many forms.

Such summaries point to the need for focusing. "Focusing" means putting emphasis on one or more points, a theme, a critical idea, and so on. The tendency for the neophyte Reality Therapist (and probably anyone learning other theories of counseling) is to allow the client to take the lead and to deal with his or her current ramblings. This is often done in order to be friends and not to appear harsh or as a listening device and trust-building technique, and it is helpful at times. But the experienced Reality Therapist possesses the added skill of being able to focus—on wants, on unfulfilled needs, on a specific day in the life of the client, on what the client can realistically achieve, and so forth. Summary and focus are used throughout the process, as are many of the other ideas contained in these guidelines.

Allow or Impose Consequences

"Allowing consequences" means that one action flows from another. To fail to study in school results in a flunking grade; to oversleep is to be late for work. Allowing consequences in counseling implies that the consequences are reasonable. Thus when the consequence is dangerous or life threatening, the therapist intervenes. As stated in the code of ethics of the American Association for Counseling and Development, "When the client's condition indicates that there is clear and imminent danger to the client or others, the member must take reasonable, personable action or inform responsible authorities" (Callas, Pope, and Depauw 1982).

Many counselors have little opportunity to "impose consequences." But some probation officers, group home workers, public assistance counselors, and the like, have ample opportunity to enforce rules and oversee the consequences of infractions. Such a position is not antithetical to the practice of Reality Therapy or to a healthy, professional relationship. Rather, the client knows boundaries and has structure. If the rules in group homes are broken, privileges are removed. If the restrictions of probation are violated, there are often severe consequences (return to the court, extended probation, arrest, and so on). Such imposition of consequences is done nonpunitively; that is, without anger or exploitation. It is a simple matter of fact that a behavior results in a consequence.

Allow Silence

The effective therapist need not feel the urgency to break every silence. Rather, it is useful at times to allow the client to take the lead in speaking first after a short period of silence. Clients thus can take responsibility for the direction of the session as well as for their Total Behaviors. Furthermore, silence allows the client to gather thoughts, gain insights, clarify pictures and perceptions, and to begin to formulate plans. Breaking this grand silence often destroys a very productive train of thought.

Be Ethical

A genuine professional relationship is founded on high ethical behavior on the part of the counselor. Conflict of interest, dual relationships (for example, sex with a client), misuse of institutional affiliations, and the like are to be avoided. Witmer (1978) suggests using a statement of professional disclosure that describes the counselor's educational background and so on. Such a statement is now required by Ohio law (1985); counselors and social workers must present their clients with a written statement containing their name, title, business address, telephone number, formal education, and areas of competence. For more detailed information, consult the codes of ethics of the various professional organizations: American Psychological Association, American Association for Counseling and Development, and National Association of Social Workers.

These guidelines, important as they are to the environment and, indeed, to the Cycle of Counseling, should nevertheless be seen as ancillary to the heart of friendship formation described in Chapter 4. As described in Chapter 1, every human being possesses needs that must be fulfilled if mental health—that is, effective control (strength)—is to be maintained. The mechanism through which needs are met is the inner world of wants, described by Glasser (1985) as a "picture album." Exploring the "picture album," as well as needs and perceptions, is a most effective means of establishing a relationship. It also constitutes the first procedure leading to change.

* 3 *

What to Avoid in a Counseling Relationship

In establishing an environment conducive to the effective use of Reality Therapy, it is important to avoid certain pitfalls. These are described in this chapter.

Don't Accept Excuses

Many trainees, teachers, and disciplinarians are delighted upon first hearing this. People beginning to learn Reality Therapy as a counseling or teaching tool have sometimes had other training in which much time and energy are spent determining the underlying reasons for clients' behaviors (that is, asking, in one form or another, the useless question "Why?" or, more specifically, "Why are you inflexible?" "Why did you fight?" "Why are you depressed?" "Why do you drink too much?" "Why are you flunking in school?" "Why do you sulk" and so on). Teachers and disciplinarians love the notion of not asking "Why." They feel that they are endlessly dealing with acted-out behaviors and have found that asking the question leads nowhere. They are most excited about having workable alternatives.

The answer to such "why" questions invariably results in a disclosure of excuses, in which control is attributed to outside

22

forces—to "them" or "to the stars" rather than to ourselves: "The reason I was fighting was that he hit me first." "I'm shy because my parents were overprotective." "I take drugs because of pressure from work." "I'm psychotic because it runs in my family." "I can't learn statistics because I never was good at math." "I'm flunking because the teachers are unfair."

It is unusual (but not unheard of) for a person to say, "I'm late for work because I didn't plan adequately." "I chose to break up my marriage." "I chose to drink myself unconscious every week." The client's having determined the excuse often leaves the helper at a loss for direction. In fact, often the helper feels the need to argue with the client so as to knock down the excuse or, the opposite, to be sympathetic. In either case progress is stopped. If therapists or teachers must defeat the excuses of clients or students, they will have an unending task. For persons who make excuses generally offer at least one more than can be nullified by even the most skillful helper. Besides, taking on the task of negating excuses shifts the responsibility from client to counselor. The latter, then, has the burden of working out the problem. In effect, the ball is in the wrong court.

To understand Reality Therapy is to understand the reasons *behind* human behavior. Consequently, there is no need to ask why people fail. All behavior springs from needs and wants. And so human beings behave—that is, drive their behavioral systems —to fulfill needs and get what they want. In Reality Therapy there is a practical assumption: people do the best they can at the time they do it. Immediately upon performing a behavior a person's opinion about the appropriateness of that specific behavior can change. But at the time the behavior was executed it seemed like the best thing to do to fulfill wants and needs. Not long ago, while driving along the expressway, I thought it was a good idea to pass the car before me. When I sped up to pass I quickly decided that it was not such a good idea. I saw a flashing red light in my mirror and instantly changed my mind. Within the next five minutes I became even more convinced that what had seemed like a good idea was, in fact, a notion that was to cost me $63.

Yet the injunction to avoid asking "why" should be understood properly. The question should be avoided only when it appears that a barrage of excuses will follow. It is valuable to ask an intellectual "why," a technical "why," or find out why a person succeeded. The essence is to avoid asking for irresponsible excuses.

Additionally, the acceptance of such excuses contains an implicit message: "You can get off the hook because you are weak and not in control of your behavior. You cannot make any changes in your life." But this is the reverse of the desirable message: "You are strong and in control of your behavior. You can change your life; you can make a better plan."

Applegate (1979) points out that there are three kinds of excuses: reasonable, frequency, and "piddling." A reasonable excuse is one that most people would agree "excuses" someone or that happens rarely; an obvious example is someone's missing work because of a death in the family. Frequency excuses are those in which the activity is performed but not as often as planned. Thus a student commits himself to study four nights and follows through on three nights. Piddling excuses are those dealt with, for the most part, in counseling. For example, the plan is not followed because the client changed his or her mind. Or someone else is blamed for the problem; children fight because "he started it." A person is late for work every day because, "I'm not a morning person." A client gambles too much because, "I have an unresolved unconscious conflict." The latter excuse is the most piddling of all!

Finally, this "don't" is often seen as one of the most helpful in the entire process. To avoid the extremes of both permissiveness and authoritarianism is an ideal sought by many teachers and counselors. This guideline skillfully provides an excellent way to be both humane and direct.

Don't Punish, Criticize, or Argue; Allow Consequences

There is much written about the differences between punishment and consequences. In summary it can be said that punishment is excessive, unrelated to the offense, for the emotional benefit of the punisher, imposed in anger, noneducational, and often elicits resentment and revenge. Consequences, on the other hand, are reasonable, are related to the offense, for the benefit of the person breaking the rule, are imposed rationally or matter of factly, are educational, and tend to result in responsible behavior and rehabilitation.

The state trooper stops the speeder, calmly asks questions, writes out the ticket, and says, "Have a nice day." The ticket is a consequence of speeding. It is a fitting inconvenience by which most drivers learn a lesson—at least for a while. (No system of even the best consequences is perfect.) If a police officer were to berate and belittle the speeders or use a nightstick on them, he would be punitive. Such treatment fits the qualities of punishment, and the result is resentment and possibly even revenge directed toward the police officer. Punishment, thus, is counterproductive because it creates frustrations and does not provide a better way to resolve them. Consequently, the person being punished continues the same, and sometimes initiates *even more* destructive behavior in order to resolve ongoing frustrations. A person humiliated by the police officer might choose to strike back violently. (Police officers are generally well aware of this, and so they administer the traffic laws calmly and cautiously!)

Criticism can be a form of punishment and should be avoided, if possible. Counselors are not likely to engage in punishment to any great degree, but they can subtly criticize. Moreover, in applying Reality Thereapy to interpersonal relationships such as marriage, it is crucial to avoid criticism. This is discussed further in Chapter 9.

There is often a question as to whether or not punishing results in softness. Parents often turn pale when they hear the phrase, "Don't punish or criticize." However, as Glasser often states, punishment is easy. It allows the person to get off the hook and avoid responsibility for future change. Consequences, administered calmly and consistently, allow less latitude for anger and recrimination. Thus when the police officer issues tickets, drivers might be upset momentarily, but in the long run they feel little resentment toward the police officer. (Obviously there are exceptions, as in the case of the excessively volatile person who engages in violent angering behaviors at the slightest provocation.)

To eliminate criticism is not an easy task. We live in a world in which criticism and its companion, angering behavior, is a national industry. To criticize is a hobby of politicians, the media, or anyone else seeking headlines. Things negative receive far more attention than positive ones. The plane crash, the auto accident, the corrupt politician, the dishonest businessperson, and the like receive constant attention. There are government agencies and company departments whose sole responsibility is to respond to and sometimes encourage criticism and negativism. National TV news shows often devote nearly all their airtime to criticizing some aspect of American life. The elimination of criticism for humankind might occur in future centuries at a later stage in our evolution. Yet the widespread use of Reality Therapy could speed up this process of human development.

On the other hand, to engage in productive critical thinking is necessary and helpful in our society. In fact, the procedure of evaluation described in Chapter 5 implies that the client "criticize" ineffective behaviors. It is obvious that even a loving parent, counselor, or friend does, in fact, criticize. And criticism can be helpful if used sparingly by a person viewed with respect and affection.

Arguing is a form of criticism. It is based on the premise that "my perceptions are better than yours." Though intellectual debates, political discussions, or athletic conversations often involve lengthy pro and con arguments about human behavior, arguing about what is good for another person is usually worthless. To argue with a child about the value of eating carrots is useless. A friendly, firm relationship characterized by the entire philosophy of Reality Therapy results in much more consumption of carrots than all the "logical" arguments of 100 million parents.

Don't Give Up Easily!

This guideline is in many ways the most difficult, in that it is hard to practice. It is easy to give up on clients who are resistant, reluctant, passive, uncooperative, angering, or apathetic. Reality Therapists keep in their own "picture albums" the image of themselves as helping the difficult client. They see themselves as helpers and clients as people capable of being helped. The motto is, "Hang in there when the going gets tough." Or, to paraphrase Robert Schuller, "Tough times never last. Tough Reality Therapists do."

Consultation, Follow-up, Continuing Education

These three guidelines, placed between the dos and don'ts in the Cycle of Counseling, are executed outside the counseling sessions. In my own teaching I have added the first—consultation —basing this suggestion on the codes of ethics that encourage supervision and consulting. It is a "Wubboldingian" step to be used or discarded according to the wish of the practitioner. It is also called "talk it over." Outside the counseling sessions the therapist seeks consultation with someone who is trained in the principles of Reality Therapy. The case can be role-played or simply discussed. For no matter how well a person practices Reality Therapy, there is room for improvement. Such improvements can take place through this consultation, or the "talk it over" guideline.

Follow-up implies later contact with the client: a phone call, a return visit, and so on. Often after termination it is useful to call the client to obtain feedback on one's own work as well as to reinforce any changes that the client has initiated.

Continuing education implies staying abreast of developments in the fields of Reality Therapy, counseling, psychology, the helping professions, and current issues. The effective Reality Therapist has an ongoing plan for professional development.

Consultation, follow-up, and continuing education constitute a thorough system for evaluating one's professional effectiveness. Thus it serves as one end of the axis linking environment and procedures (see Figure 1).

* 4 *

Procedures: Exploring the "Picture Album" (Wants), Needs, and Perceptions

1. Ask "What Do You Want?"

By means of questions revolving around this general inquiry, clients discover, define, and refine how they wish to meet their needs. They explore their "picture album," and as they respond to skillful questioning, they often learn in an insightful way many aspects of their inner world of wants that hitherto they were only vaguely aware of. They are also given the opportunity to articulate wants that they have never shared with anyone. If the counselor has developed a degree of trust, clients will open themselves, though often hesitatingly and haltingly, in ways that surprise even themselves. This question is not asked mechanically, nor on one occasion only. Rather, clients are given a chance to explore every facet of their lives—what they want from family, friends, jobs, parents, institutions. It is especially helpful to define clearly what they want from the counselor and from themselves. It is important to note that, though this exploration takes place early in the counseling process, it should continue throughout the counseling relationship because pictures change. Moreover, the clearer the picture is, the higher is the likelihood of obtaining what's wanted.

Parallel to the discussion of clients' wants is an exploration of what family, friends, and the like want from the clients. The recalcitrant teenager explores what his or her parents want from him or her. Such questions as, "What do your teachers want for you?" are useful as a prelude to the evaluation procedure described in Chapter 5. When clients are willing to work hard to improve their lives through counseling, the therapist can more easily tell them what he or she wants from them. To a husband and wife who want a better relationship, the counselor often says, "I want you to spend fifteen minutes a day doing such-and-such because this is what you say you both enjoy." (It is best, of course, to add questions designed to elicit a commitment, as in the planning and commitment procedure described in Chapter 6.)

Another facet of this exploration is to help clients elaborate on how they are getting or not getting what they want. In effect the therapist helps them describe ongoing frustrations as well as frustrations they are resolving. They thus come indirectly to the conclusion that in their behavioral systems they do, in fact, possess many behaviors that are working. Rare are the clients who are getting *nothing* of what they want.

The following hypothetical dialogue between a recalcitrant teenager and a Reality Therapist illustrates the use of this procedure described thus far. When reading this, mark in the margin your own comments about what parts of the procedure are being used (Th = therapist, Cl = client):

TH: Your parents brought you for counseling. What do they want to happen?

CL: They want me to be like my older brother.

TH: What do *you* want?

CL: I don't want nothin! Everything is fine.

TH: You don't have any problems?

CL: I wouldn't have any if they'd leave me alone.

TH: You want them to get off your back. Is that correct?

CL: You bet I do!

TH: Is there anything else you want for yourself?

CL: Whaddaya mean?

TH: For instance, do you want to graduate from school?

29

CL: Yes. In two years I'll be out of school.

TH: Do you have brothers and sisters?

CL: Two sisters and one brother.

TH: What do you want from them?

CL: ... to leave me alone.

TH: You don't want them to hassle you, put you down, borrow your things, play your stereo, etcetera?

CL: No!

TH: Do you have any close friends?

CL: Yeah!

TH: What do you expect from them?

CL: Nothing.

TH: Did you want any of them to do anything with you in the last week?

CL: Sure. One of them came over and we listened to some music.

TH: When you asked your friend to come over did you *want* him to say "yes"?

CL: Sure. That's why I asked him.

TH: So when you ask friends to do things you'd like them to say "yes."

CL: Sure.

TH: Is there anything else you want from your friends?

CL: Whaddaya mean?

TH: Do you want them to be friendly to you, call you on the phone, have fun with you?

CL: Sure, that's what friends are all about.

TH: You said you want to graduate from school. Is there anything you want from the teachers?

CL: Passing grades.

TH: Anything else?

CL: Like what?

TH: For instance, do you want them to be friendly toward you, have respect for what you think?

CL: I don't care!

TH: You mean you don't care if they're mean and nasty toward you?

CL: I want them to leave me alone and give me passing grades.

TH: Okay, so you do want two things from them. I have another question. Do you have a job?

CL: Yes. I work in a bakery on Saturdays.

TH: I assume you want to get paid for it?

CL: Uh-huh.

TH: Would you want a raise if you could get it?

CL: Yep!

TH: What would you do with double your present salary?

CL: Buy stereo tapes, video cassettes, and clothes.

TH: So you want more tapes and you want a lot of clothes? What about spending some money on a date?

CL: That'd be fine!

TH: Do you have a girlfriend?

CL: None that is steady.

TH: Would you like to go out with a girl to a dance, spend some money, drive a nice car?

CL: That'd be great. But my parents won't let me use their car.

TH: Would you use it for a date if they'd let you?

CL: Yes.

TH: Getting back to the job on Saturdays . . . do you want anything from the boss besides pay?

CL: I'd like him to be friendly.

TH: Would you like him to tell you you've done a good job once in a while?

CL: That'd be okay.

TH: Another question . . . Is there anything you want from yourself—at home, at school, in relation to your friends, on the job, etcetera?

CL: I don't know what you mean.

TH: Is there anything you'd like to do better?

CL: I'd like to learn to play the guitar.

TH: Anything else you'd like to do better?

CL: I'd like to pass in school so I don't have to go to summer school.

TH: Is there anything you want from me?

CL: I don't know.

TH: Will you think about what I could do? How I could help you figure out what you want and then get it if it's "gettable"?

CL: Yes.

TH: Okay. There are many things you've said you want: you want your parents off your back; you want to graduate from school; you want your brother and sisters to be friendly or at least leave you alone; you want your friends to call you once in a while and to be open with you; you want your teachers to treat you like a human being and treat you with respect; you want passing grades, more money, a friendly boss, more clothes, a steady girlfriend, use of the family car, and to learn to play the guitar.

The above dialogue is an attempt to illustrate how asking what a person wants can be a detailed and lengthy process. Yet this is only part of the procedure. The counselor did not explicitly and clearly distinguish between a fulfilled want and an unfulfilled want. The client wants friends to be friendly, and he does have "friendly" friends. He also wants to be "left alone," but he's not getting that. Consequently, another appropriate summary could be:

> These are some things that you want that you're already getting: you want friends that reach out to you, and they are doing that. You want a job and you have one. On the other hand, there are several areas where there could be some improvements in your life: you want less hassle from your parents, use of the family car, more money, and so forth.

Juxtaposing frustrations that clients are resolving with those that are unresolved is a very useful part of this exploration. It helps prepare the clients for further counseling, in that they see areas for needed improvement. As stated in Chapter 12, there is an implicit message which some clients are able to incorporate: that they are in control of their lives, that life can be better for them, and that there are ways to get at least part of what they want.

2. Ask "What Do You *Really* Want?"

In point 1, the recalcitrant teenager was asked to line up his wants in a horizontal fashion, side by side. He explored several separate wants in relation to his parents, teachers, himself, and so on. In point 2, clients are asked to explore their wants vertically. That is, they are asked to describe the general want which underlies the specific or surface want. The parents of the teenager might be asked what they want from their son. They might say, "good grades, to come in on time, to communicate, and to get along with the rest of the family." I have found it useful to ask about the "really want"—the underlying want—by asking, "If you had what you want, what would you have? What would life be like?" The above parent might answer, "freedom from worry," "peace of mind," "the feeling that we did a good job of raising him." When clients determine their "really wants," they are uncovering *the needs they wish to fulfill.*

As stated earlier, needs are the forces that drive all human beings. These needs are met through the fulfillment of wants ("picture album")—that is, by resolving frustrations, or closing the gap between what clients want from the environment and what they perceive they are getting. The therapist also helps clients determine what needs are being met and which remain unmet.

Incorporating point 2 into the counseling of the recalcitrant teenager could result in the following dialogue. As before, mark in the margin your own comments about this procedure:

TH: Your parents brought you for counseling. What do they want to happen?

CL: They want me to be like my older brother.

TH: What do *you* want?

CL: I don't want nothin! Everything is fine.

TH: You don't have any problems?

CL: I wouldn't have any if they'd leave me alone.

TH: You want them to get off your back. Is that correct?

CL: You bet I do!

TH: If you had what you want—your parents off your back—what would you have?

CL: I could do what I want.

TH: If you could do what you want, what would you have?

CL: Freedom from their constant lecturing.

TH: Your most basic desire is freedom?

CL: Right!

TH: And you don't have nearly so much as you want?

CL: Right again!

TH: What about school? What do you want from the school?

CL: In two years I'll be out of school.

TH: Do you want to graduate with a diploma?

CL: Yes.

TH: If you had the diploma, how would life be better than if you dropped out?

CL: I could get a job.

TH: And if you have the job, what would you have?

CL: I'd have money to do what I want.

TH: And what would more money, even an unlimited supply, enable you to do?

CL: I could do what I want!

TH: And not have to rely on other people?

CL: Yes, I would not depend on them.

TH: You'd be totally independent, stand on your own two feet without answering to anyone?

CL: That's it exactly.

TH: That sure sounds like total freedom to me. Is that what it means to you?

CL: You bet!

In this dialogue the therapist attempts to help the client identify the more general want and then the fundamental need which he is seeking to satisfy. The groundwork is thus laid for helping him get what he *really* wants, in the event that he cannot attain his present want. He has thus been helped to replace one unattainable picture in his inner "picture album" with a more attainable, realistic one. This replacement, though sometimes a difficult job, is done through the use of subsequent procedures in the counseling process.

3. Ask "What Do You Think People Want from You?"

With this question, clients are asked how they view the world as it affects them. They examine the expectations of their family, friends, schools, co-workers, supervisors, society in general, and so on. They are also asked what they are willing to do and what they are *not* willing to do to live according to these expectations. The counselor, for the most part, remains nonjudgmental about either their willingness or their unwillingness to change. Many questions are asked in order to help clients look at the expectations (wants) of other people: "What do your parents expect from you in relation to your schoolwork?" "What time does your boss want you to come to work?" "What do you want that is the same as what your parents want?" "Your boss's wants?" "What are some wants that are different from what these people expect of you?" Again, clients are asked about what they *really* want—their fundamental need underlying the picture. "What would your family, job, and so on be like if your wants and their wants matched?"

At this point it is also useful to help clients look at their willingness to work for the fulfillment of *some* of their pictures. "Since your parents want so many things from you, what are you willing to give them, what are you willing to do, what will you settle for?"

Incorporating point 3 into the counseling of our recalcitrant teenager might produce dialogue such as follows. Again, mark in the margin your own comments:

TH: What do your parents want from you?
CL: I told you. They want me to be like my older brother.
TH: Anything else?
CL: To come in early, give up my friends, pass in school.
TH: What do you think your teachers want?
CL: They want me to behave better.
TH: Like how?
CL: Come to class on time. But they are always on my back!
TH: But they want you to be there on time and study also?
CL: Yes.
TH: If you did all these things, what would your life be like?
CL: I don't know; I never tried it.
TH: Are you willing to change anything in your life? Anything you do?
CL: Like what?

4. Ask "How Do You Look at It?"

Up to this point we have helped clients explore their "picture albums," along with both their resolved and unresolved frustrations. We now explore the storehouse of perceptions—that is, what has been filtered from the external world. Clients are asked to describe whether they view the situation from a high (value) level or a low (recognition) level of perception. In the example of how the parents might view the recalcitrant teenager, they could be asked, "How do you see your son?" "When you look at him what do you see?" "What are you able to accept and what upsets you?" "What does he do that you approve of?" "Disapprove of?" "What do you disapprove of that you can live with?" "What does he do that makes no difference to you?"

The purpose of this questioning is to prepare for more counseling and for the application of other procedures. Subsequently, clients will be asked if they want to change the direction of their lives. They will be asked if what they are doing is helping or hurting, and if their present direction is satisfactory to them. They will be asked to make plans to improve their own behaviors.

The following dialogue is continued from that immediately earlier. As usual, make your own comments in the margin:

TH: Are you willing to change anything in your life? Anything you do?

CL: Like what?

TH: Like how you look at your parents or the school?

CL: I don't know!

TH: How do you look at things now? For instance, how do you see yourself at home?

CL: I live there.

TH: Do you see yourself as giving or only as "getting" from the family?

CL: I don't get much.

TH: Could be . . . but do you see yourself as trying to make life easier for those around you?

36

CL: Not much!

TH: How about school? How do you see your teacher? Is there anyone you regard as helpful?

CL: How do you mean?

TH: Is there anyone you like—even a little?

CL: Well . . . there is my science teacher. . . .

A question that runs through this exchange is, "Do you want to change?" "Do you want to change what you want . . . how do you look at it?" and so on. Such questions are geared to the specific person, of course. Thus the parents who might see their teenager as a "lazy, rule-breaking, uncommunicative, flunking pot-head" would be asked, "Do you want to change your opinion of him?" The teenager in question is asked, "Do you want to change the way you see your teacher, your parents?" and so on. At this point the response is not as significant as the mere fact that they are *asked* such questions. The asking is important, for up to a point this procedure is one of exploration. Also, as stated in Chapter 12, there is a message contained in these questions: that clients have control over the pain they suffer; that they can change their lives for the better. Such questions serve also to establish the client-counselor relationship; that is, they provide a structure through which the relationship can develop. They also pave the way for future questioning.

5. Tell Them What You Have to Offer, What You Want from Them, How You Look at the Situation

In my counseling, I make the following points in the first session: (1) there are no guarantees about "cures"; (2) the content of therapy is confidential; (3) financial details are discussed; (4) my professional qualifications are disclosed; (5) a brief explanation of Reality Therapy is given (I can help them feel better, get at least some of the things they want, and so forth, on the condition that they are willing to work at it). I add that there are two general kinds of counseling: "do" counseling and "talk" counseling. I offer them "do" counseling. We will talk—a lot. But their improvement depends not only on talk, but on what they are willing to do outside the counseling. Thus they understand that I believe they have strength and control, and they have within them the power to gain even more. They are also congratulated for seeking help. This effort illustrates that they now have some strength and that they want to improve their lives.

6. Get a Commitment to Counseling

An important part of the procedure is to elicit a commitment to counseling. This commitment follows quite naturally when the therapist explains the benefits of the relationship. It is made more explicit by simple questions such as, "Are you willing to work hard at the problem?" "Do you think we can work together on this?" "How much effort and energy will you put into changing things?" and so on.

Finally, it must be emphasized that this procedure means "to establish as soon as possible, a warm, supportive relationship, and throughout therapy to insist that clients take a hard look at the life they are choosing to lead. Unless this kind of friendship is woven deeply into the fabric of therapy from beginning to end, the helping process will rarely be effective" (Glasser 1980).

* 5 *

Procedures: Exploring Total Behavior and Evaluating

Total Behavior

It is well to discuss early in the counseling process the overall direction that clients are taking, where they are going, where the behavior (Doing or Acting, Thinking, Feeling) is taking them. This is preliminary to the subsequent evaluation of whether it is a desirable direction. Even if clients cannot articulate this clearly, and many cannot, it is well to explore the subject. With such questioning, the therapist figuratively holds up a mirror before the client and asks, "What do you see for yourself now and in the future?" It takes time for the reflection to become clear to clients and for them to find words to express what they perceive.

Ask "What Are You Doing?"

The global question about the direction of the client's life is useful but insufficient as a complete procedure. As the encounter between counselor and client develops, it is necessary to be more specific, to focus on unique, precise, moment-to-moment actions that determine the overall direction.

So important is this question that the classic book of cases on Reality Therapy is called *What Are You Doing?* (Glasser 1980). To some extent this procedure is inseparable from the "Be Friends" component of Reality Therapy, for another way to make friends and to enter the inner world of clients is to ask them how they choose to live their daily lives, how they spend their time—that is, how they are driving their behavioral system to resolve frustrations (get what they want) and to fulfill their needs. In this procedure each word is important.

"What"

Clients are asked exactly how they spend their time. The key is to be as precise as possible. A helpful technique is to ask the client to imagine his or her mind as a television camera which records every detail of a specific day (such as the previous day). It is important to elicit a *specific* day rather than a *typical* day. A description of a typical day will not include specific, unique details so important to this self-examination. This process of having the client describe a specific day or part of a day could take a considerable length of time, since every facet is explained. What exact time did the client get up? What kind of breakfast was eaten? Was anyone present? Were any words spoken? What was said? What exactly was done after breakfast? The client's description is that of a television camera recording events that are unique, precise, detailed, and never-to-be-repeated exactly the same way. Applegate (1979) emphasizes that such a description could take forty-five to sixty minutes, or even longer.

In this procedure the counselor is able to enter the world of the client and identify those areas in which the client is in control and those in which there is little control, as well as behaviors about which the client will subsequently make evaluations, or value judgments. Another purpose of exploring the "what" is that it is a way of holding the figurative behavioral mirror before a client, asking the person to look at him or herself in a specific way. Analogously, it is more effective to look in the mirror to discover that you forgot to comb your hair than it is for someone simply to tell you. To see it yourself is more impressive and requires more self-examination.

"Are"

In asking for a description of Doing behaviors, *current* behaviors are emphasized. In Reality Therapy we stress how clients attempt to fulfill needs as life is lived today, or currently. The past is important, and in many ways it explains how we arrived at our present situation. As Glasser (1980) says, "Everything we do today is in some way related to everything that has happened to us since birth. But since we can only correct for today and plan for a better tomorrow, we talk little about the past—we can't undo anything that has already occurred." The root of current problems and disturbances, thus, is in the present *more* than in the past. Though a client's problems may have started in the past, his or her unfulfilled want or need exists *now* and must be resolved *now* and fulfilled *now*. This is indeed a controversial point among many professional persons, as evidenced in the way some disturbances are treated in various therapeutic methods.

Thus the disturbance labeled Post-Vietnam Syndrome is often believed to be caused *now* by the past Vietnam experience. From the point of view of Reality Therapy, the behaviors associated with this syndrome are caused by lingering unmet wants and needs which exist *now*. Vietnam veterans have received little recognition for their service in Vietnam. On the other hand, after World War II there was an enormous outpouring of love and recognition for veterans. The earlier veterans received a hero's welcome, quite the opposite of the situation with Vietnam veterans. For a while they were criticized, given unflattering labels, and cut off from benefits which they feel they deserve. After the Second World War, many veterans were able to spend weeks rehashing "war stories," and in that sense having fun as they traveled homeward on troop ships. Vietnam veterans, on the other hand, were often home forty-eight hours after being in the jungles of Vietnam. This shock, coupled with rejection or often, at best, apathy and stony silence, has resulted in many unmet wants (frustrations) and unmet needs for Vietnam veterans. Some (not all by any means!) have attempted to drive the behavioral system by drinking, depression, psychosis, family violence, and other destructive actions. These behaviors are attempts to resolve frustration and to fulfill unmet needs that exist *now*. The *cause* of the behaviors exists in the present, and consequently, heavy emphasis is laid on the question, "What *are* you doing?"

Because of this emphasis on the present, it could mistakenly be concluded that the Reality Therapist refuses to discuss the past. However, as Glasser (1980) states, "We are not trained to be rigid in any way." Thus it is acceptable to discuss past history. The most useful history is positive experience, so past successes are stressed. For example, depressed clients are asked about a time in the past when they were not depressed. Again, clients should describe what they were doing when they felt good. Marriage partners who are not getting along are asked about times when they were happy together. The description must be specific, not vague or general. Clients should answer questions such as, "What exactly were you doing? When? Where? With whom? What needs were you fulfilling when you were doing the activity?"

"You"

In asking, "What are *you* doing?" the therapist focuses on what the *client* is doing. At first glance, this point appears obvious. Yet with many clients it is sometimes necessary to make a special effort to explain that it is imperative they describe their own Doing behavior, rather than that of someone else. Applegate (1980) points out that, in marriage counseling, clients prefer to discuss the other person's behavior. The skillful counselor focuses on each person's Doing behavior and what he or she is willing to change. This focusing is not as easy as it first appears. Resistance is often strong at this point. The dialogue with the recalcitrant teenager, begun in Chapter 4, for instance, might continue as follows:

TH: What did you say to your mother yesterday?
CL: All she did was gripe at me.

TH: But what did *you* say?

CL: She kept hassling me about school.

TH: Did you talk to her?

CL: Yes. But it wasn't my fault. She started the argument.

TH: That might be . . . but what did *you* say to her during the argument?

CL: I told her to stick it!

TH: Anything else?

CL: She started it!

TH: But what else did *you* say to her?

CL: I told her to go to hell.

TH: What was her reaction?

CL: She got madder, screamed at me, and cried . . . then left the room.

TH: What did you choose to do then?

CL: I went to my room and stayed there for the rest of the day.

The dialogue illustrates the therapist's efforts to focus on the *client's* behavior rather than on that of the mother. This procedure does not exclude asking about other people. However, this procedure, and all the others described in this book, is not a rigid prescription to be adhered to in an inflexible manner. The therapist even asks about the behavior of the mother. But the *focus* and emphasis are clear: What did *you* (the client) do?

"Doing"

In this procedure, the Doing component of the behavioral system is explored. This detailed discussion of the Doing (or Acting) component is significant and controversial for therapists who have a more nondirective style and theory.

In many counseling approaches, training programs, and self-help workshops, the counselor and client are encouraged to discuss feelings. This is based on the assumption that feelings are at the root of problems or are the source of motivation. And so it is important to identify and label the feelings, to "get in touch with" the feelings, and to gain "insight" into their source, which is often seen as a past experience sometimes dating back many years.

43

Reality Therapists take a different view, however. Rather than putting feelings at the root of Doing behaviors, they are seen as the natural accompaniment of the Doing aspect of the total behavior the client has chosen. If a student is anxious about procrastinating the preparation for exams, it is evident that the anxieting is the natural companion of the ineffective Doing behaviors. The effective therapist helps such a person examine what he or she wants and is doing to get it. (These two efforts culminate in formulating an action plan.)

In examining the role of feelings, it is important to realize that human motivation does not begin with behavior. Rather, in Reality Therapy motivation is seen to be rooted in unresolved frustrations: the gaps between what we want and what we get which, when closed, result in need fulfillment. Thus Feeling, which is an inseparable part (more accurately an "aspect") of total behaviors (the other aspects are Doing and Thinking), is generated to close the gaps (resolve frustration) and fulfill needs. Consequently, depressing, angering, and "upset" feelings are a major part of our efforts to mold the external world so that we get what we want. And so, feelings are not a source of motivation. Human beings do not act *primarily* to feel better. They act and feel and think (that is, they generate total behaviors) in order to get what they want. Fulfilling wants and needs results in better feelings, actions, and thoughts.

Finally, it must be emphasized that feelings are very important in the theory and practice of Reality Therapy. They serve as warning lights, as do the red lights on the dashboard of an automobile. When the lights go on, the driver realizes that something in the mechanism is malfunctioning. It is of no use to talk endlessly about the lights, but it is helpful to take effective action to solve the problem. The causes of the "red lights" in the human mechanism may be manifested by total behaviors that are generated in the behavioral system but, of course, they fundamentally come from unfulfilled wants and unmet needs. Thus the good Reality Therapist does, indeed, "get to the root of the problem."

This rather abstract point can best be elucidated with several examples. If a person is hungry or tired, it will do little good to spend time discussing or "getting in touch" with these feelings;

counseling would be a waste of time! In fact, such a client might quickly decide to take action on his or her own. The hungry person could easily leave the session to eat a hamburger; the tired person might handle the problem of fatigue simply by falling asleep! Similarly, the person who is nervousing or worrying about a speech to be given is best helped by a Do-plan—for example, practicing the speech. A grieving person is best helped by recognizing the unmet want and the unfulfilled need, as well as by making Doing plans to fulfill needs and wants. These are examples that require various levels of therapeutic skill. To help a person get a hamburger is, to put it mildly, rather basic—so basic that counseling is rarely needed. (In twenty years of counseling, I have never had a client who complained of hunger or fatigue and didn't know what to do about it.) The grieving person, on the other hand, might require months—more likely *years*—to fulfill wants and needs. Many such people carry the loss with them for decades, never replacing the relationship. Consequently, they continue to generate total behaviors imprinted with mourning.

Still, this reasoning explains only theoretically the purpose of emphasizing daily Doing behaviors in counseling. Unfortunately, not all clients have read books on Reality Therapy or have attended training workshops. They come to counseling not only feeling bad, but with the idea that talking about the pain will cure it or that the therapist can give them some psychological medicine that will work to effect a cure. Very often they feel that the pain is caused by outside sources and that they are not responsible for it. The recalcitrant teenager might say, "My mother aggravates me," "She makes me mad!," "My teacher flunked me." Clients (and people in general) are less inclined to deny that they choose the Doing component of the behavior. The teenager can hardly deny that he chose to argue, to go to his room, to refuse to eat, and to fail to study for the exam. Therefore, since Reality Therapy is based on the principle that behaviors are chosen, it is more helpful to discuss the component that clients will more readily admit to choosing—that is, over which they have control. Our teenager will more readily admit power over his choice to go to his room, and so on, than control over his angry feelings. Therefore with many clients, especially those who are cooperative and willing, it is useful to explain the theory; that when they change the Doing aspect of their behavior—that is, make better choices—they will necessarily change the Feeling component, too. For the Doing component is more tangible, more measurable, more easily planned. A client cannot "plan" to feel enthusiastic in the morning. Planning to exercise for five minutes or to sing in the shower is more precise, more tangible, and more measurable. A plan to overcome anger is vague, imprecise, and not measurable; a plan to keep the voice low instead of raised in argument is a Do-plan. Thus, one of the reasons for discussing the Doing aspect of behavior is that effective plans (see Chapter 6) can be made more easily. And so, in Reality Therapy, the Doing component is stressed in the counseling process more than the other components.

Following is a segment of a hypothetical conversation between the therapist and our resistant teenager, in which the therapist attempts to focus on the Doing component.

TH: What did you say to your mother yesterday?

CL: All she did was gripe at me.

TH: Give me the details—that is, one example.

CL: She hassled me about school.

TH: When was this and where did it happen?

CL: After school.

TH: What time?

CL: About three forty-five.

TH: Where were you? What part of the house?

CL: In the living room.

TH: Were you standing, sitting? Give me the details.

CL: I walked in the door. I was standing.

TH: Where was she?

CL: She was in the dining room at the table going through some papers.

TH: Who spoke first?

CL: I did.

TH: What did you say?

46

CL: I said, "I'm going over to Davy's house."

TH: What did she say?

CL: She said, "What about your schoolwork?"

TH: How did you answer?

CL: I said, "What about it?"

TH: In what tone of voice?

CL: Kinda sarcastic. She makes me mad everytime she opens her mouth!

TH: She *forces* you to get angry.

CL: Yeah!

TH: Okay. We'll come back to that! After your sarcastic comeback, what did she say?

CL: She said I was not to go out, but had to stay home and study.

TH: What did you say and do?

CL: I told her I was going out because I didn't have any schoolwork.

TH: And then?

CL: She told me to stay at home.

TH: Keep going. I'm listening.

CL: I went up to my room.

TH: Did you go in a good mood to your room?

CL: Hell no! I was mad.

TH: I'll bet you were furious, even red in the face.

CL: I was really, really mad.

TH: What were you thinking at that moment?

CL: I'd like to slug her!

TH: Man! *Rage* is the word.

CL: That's about it.

TH: Did you go quietly or noisily?

CL: I don't know!

TH: Did you stomp up and slam the door?

CL: Yes, I guess so!

TH: Plop down on the bed?

CL: Yeah.

TH: What about the stereo?

CL: I turned it on loud.

47

In this example the therapist helps the client describe in detail a specific incident, with emphasis on the Doing component. At the same time, he alludes to Feeling and Thinking behaviors. It was stated earlier that the Doing component (sometimes also referred to as the Acting component) of behavior is emphasized and stressed. Nevertheless, since behavior always involves Doing (Acting), Thinking, Feeling, and Physiology (not emphasized in this book), it is perfectly acceptable to discuss all aspects with clients. But, as in the example just given, Feeling, Thinking, and Physiology are linked with the Doing aspect of behavior. Thus behavior is *seen* as "total," discussed initially as a unit, as in the earlier part of this chapter, and then discussed later in some detail, emphasizing the Doing element but not omitting the other aspects. Perhaps you can think of other specific questions which would help the client identify his exact actions. The therapist needs to think of his or her own mind as a television camera recording specific events. The client can also be asked to imagine him- or herself as a television camera, omitting no detail.

It is clear, then, that the purpose of this description is to focus on the component of behavior that is most easily changed and which the client will most readily admit to choosing—and, paradoxically, which the client might be least aware of.

The fact that we tend to be less aware of the Doing aspects of our behavior than of our feelings (when we are frustrated) is yet another reason why Reality Therapists emphasize the Doing rather than the Feeling component in counseling dialogues. At first glance, it might appear that we are most conscious of our Doing component, yet a few examples serve to illustrate how we are least aware of it. Most of us have at one time or another attended a lecture during which the speaker continually jiggled the change in his pocket. The speaker was aware of feelings, perhaps nervousness, but only marginally aware of the Doing component of his behavioral system. Similarly, you've probably experienced an argument with another member of your family. If you had to drive somewhere afterwards you might have been upset and arrived at your destination without being aware of how you got there. Why? You were aware of your Feeling and Thinking behaviors but less aware of your Doing behaviors. There are many other such examples from daily life that serve to illustrate this point.

Though it is perfectly acceptable to discuss all aspects of behavior, skillful questioning can help a client become aware of the Doing behaviors. Thus in our hypothetical dialogue, the teenager is hesitant to answer questions about whether he went to his room quietly or noisily. He really doesn't know without some reflection. When frustrated, he—like all of us—is less aware of the Doing aspect than of the Feeling and Thinking components.

For all of these reasons the Doing, or Acting, component of total behavior is emphasized in this procedure. In our example of a therapist-client discussion, there is a clear effort to avoid the subsequent procedures. It might seem to be a stilted dialogue, but the purpose of these hypothetical transcripts is not to illustrate artful counseling, but to show each procedure in the process of Reality Therapy.

The prominence given to the Doing component does not exclude a more thorough discussion of the client's thoughts. Often there are times when a discussion of thoughts accompanying the Doing and Feeling components can be most useful. As stated in the discussion of "*are*" earlier, a powerful procedure is to ask clients to conduct a searching self-evaluation. Yet it is usually necessary first to explore their mental behaviors. Appropriate questions around the Thinking component include the following examples: "What did you tell yourself when you did such and such?" "What do you think will happen if you make that decision?" "Do you think you can handle the situation?" A dialogue with our difficult teenager, in which this component is emphasized, will take a slightly different direction from that related earlier:

TH: What did you say to your mother yesterday?
CL: All she did was gripe at me.
TH: What thoughts went through your mind when she griped at you?
CL: I hated her.
TH: Did you use those words in your thoughts?
CL: Yes. I thought, "I hate you, you bitch!"

49

TH: Did you choose any other thoughts?

CL: "I told her to . . ."

TH: When was the last time you chose to have some positive thoughts about your mother?

CL: I don't remember any. All she does is bitch at me!

TH: Maybe when you were small?

CL: She used to help me with my homework when I was young.

TH: What positive thoughts did you choose at that time?

CL: I thought of her as helpful.

In this example the therapist emphasizes questions that do not overlap with a previous or a subsequent procedure. In the actual practice of Reality Therapy it is difficult and even unnecessary to separate the perceptual levels from the Thinking component and to separate the Thinking component from evaluation. Value judgments about the effectiveness of efforts provide a spark which ignites a change in both Doing and Thinking behaviors.

Asking for Evaluations (Value Judgments)

For many therapists this procedure appears to be the simplest, most obvious, and most automatic. Yet practice shows it is the most subtle and the most easily skipped. In asking for evaluations from clients, it is crucial that the value judgments are made by the *clients* rather than by the counselor. In Reality Therapy the therapist can feel free to offer opinions and judgments about client effectiveness, but these are of little value if the client doesn't first and foremost make those judgments. Through skillful questioning, the therapist helps clients evaluate their behavior in seven ways, and then evaluates his or her own performance in three ways.

1. Ask, "Is Your Behavior Helping or Hurting You." The most fundamental form of evaluation is for the therapist to ask clients whether they believe their behavior serves their best interests— that is, is it leading them in the most desirable direction now or in the future? This form of value judgment elicited from the client is a starting point. By itself, it is useful in the initial stage of therapy. But as the relationship develops and as progress begins, it is necessary to be more specific and more precise about value judgments. It is by means of small, measurable behaviors that the direction of a client's life is changed or improved.

In addition, many persons who enter counseling need not change the entire direction of their lives. They might merely wish to make a "fine-tuning" change. Nevertheless, it is useful to start with this generic evaluative question.

2. Ask, "Is What You're Doing Helping You Get What You Want?" After determining whether a global directional change is needed or a fine-tuning adjustment is more advantageous, it is necessary to proceed to more specific evaluations. In this value judgment, the client looks at specific behaviors to determine if current Doing behavior is effective in fulfilling wants and needs. For instance, a depressing person who had been laid off his job for several months described his present Doing behavior: "Yesterday I got up at 11:00 A.M., ate, watched TV, visited with a neighbor who stopped by in the afternoon, watched TV in the evening, and went to bed." The value-judgment question is, "Does sitting around and not exercising help you to feel good, help you to stay in shape, or give you added energy to get out and apply for a job?" Thus the client is asked to judge whether current Doing behaviors are effective in getting what he wants. This form of value-judgment question is the most frequently used. And like all the questioning in this procedure, it is based on extensive discussion of wants, perceptions, and total behaviors. The client should have identified unfulfilled wants and needs previously, as well as described in detail the current Doing behaviors.

3. Ask, "Is What You're Doing Against the Rules?" Is it acceptable behavior? When the client breaks rules or in any way presents a discipline problem, the counselor (or parent) does not ask, "Is it helping?" or, "Is it realistic?" For example, if someone has been fighting, the answer is usually, "Of course, it helped. He won't slug me again!" The client still sees the behavior as helpful and attainable. Consequently, it is more useful simply to ask *if such behavior is acceptable.* This was the approach taken by a police officer when he pulled me over as I was driving on the expressway. I had accelerated to pass a slower car. The police officer asked me, "How fast were you going?" I answered, "Sixty-five miles an hour." He replied, "What is the speed limit?" Difficult as it was, I replied, "Fifty-five miles per hour." The words stuck in my throat and emerged only after a seemingly endless amount of time. The importance of this procedure, especially in rule-breaking behavior, is not that clients learn new information, but it is rather as if they look in a mirror and observe their own Doing behaviors. It is crucial that they look in such a mirror, because people are least aware of the Doing component of their behavioral system.

This procedure is done repeatedly, since it is rare that a person changes behavior with one such confrontation. As Cornell (1986) points out, the consistent use of these procedures in an institution produces visible results. Also, it should be emphasized that, in the context of rule-breaking behaviors, conventional wisdom assumes that it is easier to be aware of the Doing component rather than the Feeling or Thinking components. And yet, as stated earlier, the opposite is true. When I first began my high-school teaching career, I was very much aware of my feelings of nervousing, anxieting, and so on. But I was unaware of how these manifested themselves in the Doing component until some students approached me and begged that I stop pacing back and forth and stop jiggling the change in my pocket! Similarly, there is an expression, usually directed toward children when they are carrying a soft drink, pouring milk, or doing something that requires clear attending to the Doing component: "Watch what you are doing!" They are aware of feelings and thoughts, but only marginally aware of their Doing component. Likewise, many automobile accidents are caused by "mental lapses"—that is, not being aware of the Doing component of the behavioral system; the driver is "lost in thought," not paying attention to the driving (Doing component).

The focus on Doing rather than Feeling as a point of emphasis

in Reality Therapy is controversial among counselors and therapists who are trained in other methods. Such methods stress a
discussion of feelings on the assumption that they are at the root
of Doing behaviors, the source of motivation, and so forth. Reality Therapy is based on the premise that the component most
under people's direct control is the Doing one. This point was
discussed previously and is reemphasized here because it often
appears to the observer of the rule-breaking person that the latter
"should be aware of what they're doing." They can become
aware of what they are doing by skillful questioning, but until
then they are less aware of it than they are of what they feel or
think.

4. *Ask, "Is What You Want Realistic or Attainable?"* The
fourth form of value-judgment questioning revolves around the
attainability of wants. Clients are asked to evaluate whether what
they want is realistic. We return to our recalcitrant teenager:

TH: What do you want from your parents?
CL: I want them to leave me alone.
TH: Do you think they will do that?
CL: They ought to! I just wanna be left alone! Why do I have to
do what they want?
TH: Parents are like that sometimes. But my question is, do you
think they will leave you alone to come and go, to use their
house, etcetera, not demand anything from you, or not have
any rules for you?
CL: I guess not.
TH: Let's put it another way. Let's say they spend $500 per
month on you for room, food, clothes, education, and all
the things you need now, in addition to the thousands of
dollars they spent on you when you were growing up. They
have quite an investment in you. Are they going to ignore
this investment? Not to mention whether they care about
you as a son.
CL: I guess they're going to watch me closely.
TH: Maybe even make rules that you think are ridiculous?
CL: Yeah. I guess you're right.

53

The counselor does not argue about whether the want is attainable or reasonable, or whether the parents' rules are fair. The focus in this situation is on whether the want of the client is something that can be fulfilled. Counselors using this procedure, as well as all the others, clearly play a directive role by taking the lead with skillful and precise questioning.

5. *Ask, "Does It Help You to Look at it That Way?"* The fifth value judgment to be made by the client and elicited by the therapist relates to the way the client sees the world. This is best illustrated by the following dialogue with our young friend. It could well follow immediately upon the preceding value judgment about the attainability of wants:

TH: How do you look at your parents? What do you see when you look at them?

CL: A couple of bitches.

TH: What do they do that leads you to say that?

CL: They are always yelling at me.

TH: So you see them as your enemies!

CL: You bet I do.

TH: You see them as people you dislike, maybe even want to get away from . . . as people who are against you?

CL: Yeah.

TH: Does it really help you to see them so negatively?

CL: That's the way they are!

TH: When did you see them more favorably?

CL: When I was about two years old!

TH: Did you see them as friends?

CL: Yeah.

TH: Did you feel better then or now?

CL: Then.

TH: Regardless of how they "really are," does it help you more to see them as enemies or as friends?

CL: I can't change how I look at them as long as they treat me unfairly.

TH: I'm not saying you should change. I'm only asking you

whether your view of them as your enemies really helps you to feel good.

CL: I felt better a few years ago when I looked at them as friends.

In this exchange the therapist has asked the teenager to determine his perceptual level and to evaluate it. The teenager views his parents at a high perceptual level, making judgments (nearly all negative) about him. Subsequently, the therapist might attempt to assist the teenager to lower his perceptual level—to see his parents simply as people, with whom he lives—and not as enemies. This is not done easily. But it can be accomplished if behavior, especially the Doing component, is changed. This will be discussed in more detail in Chapter 6.

6. *Ask, "How Committed Are You to the Process of Therapy and to Changing Your Life?"* And, "Is the present level of commitment going to work to your advantage?" The sixth value judgment is an attempt to help the client make genuine efforts to work hard at resolving problems and taking better control. Like the other forms of evaluation, this self-examination by the client is ongoing, occurring throughout the process of counseling. The therapist, listening carefully for various levels of commitment, observes that the levels are sometimes stated explicitly by the client. At other times they are implied. The counselor should listen carefully and try to elicit a higher level of commitment. There are five levels of commitment. Beginning with the lowest level, they are as follows:

1. "I don't really want to be here. Someone forced me to come. I don't want to change. It's not my problem." Such clients are frequently referred by spouses, parents, courts, etc. They do not accept ownership for the problem but project responsibility onto others.
2. "I want the pleasure resulting from change, but I do not want to make the effort." Clients with this level of commitment often are willing to make plans but

fail to follow through. An overweight person might want to lose weight but often chooses to do nothing about it. An unhappy spouse wants to have a better marital relationship but decides that efforts toward quality time are not worth the effort.

3. "I'll try." Clients often make a level of commitment to achieve results that builds in the seeds of failure. To "try to get more exercise," while often a good start, is to allow for both success and for no results. One can succeed at trying but fail at doing. To "try" to study harder is not the same as actually turning off the TV, saying "no" to friends, and sitting in front of the book reading and taking notes. Still, this level of commitment is evidence of a genuine desire to change and can be readily escalated to a higher level of commitment.

4. "I'll do my best." This high level of commitment to therapy is indicative of a motivational level that a counselor can build on. Such a client shows an intense desire to change.

5. "I'll do whatever it takes." This highest level of commitment leaves little room for escape to excuse making and failure. It is a very firm commitment and the one toward which the counselor aims in eliciting a promise from the client to work hard.

In listening for the various levels of commitment to counseling the counselor diagnoses the level and then helps the client raise it so that change can be brought about in the briefest time possible. In the diagnosis it is important not only to listen for words but to attend to non-verbal behavior such as tone of voice. Also, follow-up sessions are used to determine the client's ongoing degree of commitment to change.

7. Ask, "Is It a Helpful Plan?" This portion of the evaluation procedure occurs after the planning procedure and could also be listed as part of the commitment procedure. After the client makes a plan there is a determination as to whether it meets the criteria for an effective plan: whether it is need-fulfilling, simple, attainable, and so on. These criteria will be discussed in the next chapter.

Finally, evaluation is seen as the lower end of the axis connecting procedures and environment. Therapists also evaluate their specific behavior relative to clients, their own general competencies, and their own professional growth. These evaluations are accomplished by follow-up to various counseling sessions, consultation with other professionals, and continuing education (see Figure 1).

Such self-evaluation serves as a foundational element upon which is built successful counseling, and so, serves as an important component in a counseling environment. Ethical and conscientious counselors follow up their counseling sessions by keeping their own commitments to clients, by being prompt, and so forth. They seek specific consultation when they perceive a limitation, and they attend workshops, classes, and professional meetings designed to provide more therapeutic knowledge and skill. This three-fold approach of follow-up, consultation, and continuing education thus helps the therapist provide an environment conducive to effective counseling (see Figure 1).

* 6 *

Procedures: Planning and Commitment

A Positive Plan of Action

If evaluation is the keystone of the therapy structure, planning makes the structure functional. It puts the finishing touch on the counseling process. A plan that fulfills wants and needs is the target for this entire method of counseling. A client gains more effective control over his or her life with plans that have the following characteristics.

Need-Fulfilling

The plan should, at least implicitly, be tied to a need in the counseling. If a plan to play cards or golf is not fun for a client, the plan will be meaningless and will not be carried out on any regular basis. A plan to call a disagreeable person will often not be followed because it damages the client's need for belonging. Of course, if there is a more important, need-fulfilling payoff, the client might follow through. For instance, an unemployed person might call a prospective employer, thereby taking the risk of feeling rejected, if there is the chance of getting the job and thus fulfilling the need for power or achievement. A skillful counselor aims at helping clients follow through on plans that at first appear disagreeable by linking such plans to a greater need-fulfilling payoff. A depressing person might dread facing the day, rising early to take a brisk walk, making a phone call, or cleaning the house. A gentle push can be helpful if it is based on the hope (in the client's mind) that a better life is possible. Resistance, discussed in detail in Chapter 6, is handled by the therapist's reverting back to the earlier procedures: for example, "Do you really want to overcome the depression?" "Is lying around in bed helping you to feel better or to overcome the depression?" The key question that can be answered by the client centers on what the plan will do for him or her; that is, what would be the internal short-term or long-term effect (fulfilled need) that could result from successfully carrying out the plan?

Simple

A simple, easy-to-understand plan is the best plan. Such simplicity is, of course, geared to the individual. Some clients can fill a notebook with detailed plans that, for them, are simple and easy to understand. But for others, a one-shot plan takes enormous effort and is a major success. A very depressing person whom I once counseled was strong enough to make the following plan: on her way home she was to tell her daughter, the driver of the car, "The river is beautiful." Such a plan was simple and un-complicated, but nevertheless was a major step forward for this woman who had been making depressing choices for a long pe-riod of time.

Simple plans are especially important with people who are seriously depressing, angering, resenting, or wallowing in any negative feelings. They are very much aware of their feelings and only marginally aware of their Doing behaviors. Consequently, after they become aware of their Doing behaviors, they gradually change these behaviors through simple, easy-to-understand plans. Thus the simpler the plan, the better for clients who are consumed by their negative Feeling behaviors.

Realistic and Attainable

The example just mentioned, in which the client says, "The river is beautiful," also illustrates the importance of helping clients make plans that are attainable. The achievability is based not only on the client's degree of awareness of the Doing component of the behavioral system, but on his or her degree of strength. The effective Reality Therapist has made an earlier assessment as to the strength of the client. At this point, whether the client is ready to make a minimal plan or a more detailed and extensive one should have been determined.

It is important to recognize that even a small plan which helps the client realize there is hope can be a significant step forward. A tiny plan might seem like a trifle, but there is no such thing as an insignificant plan. G. K. Chesterton once remarked that trifles make perfection and perfection is no trifle. A minimal, or "insignificant," plan helps clients realize that they can take better charge of their lives, that they can improve their surroundings, that they can feel success, and that they need not be consumed by destructive choices. The often-quoted Japanese proverb, "A journey of a thousand miles is begun with one step," applies here.

Something To Do; Not To Stop Doing

We have all heard someone proclaim, "My New Year's resolution is to stop smoking . . . to stop yelling . . . to stop oversleeping." Such statements violate many of the characteristics of a good plan, including that it should be positive. The behavioral system is constantly functioning. Even during sleep, part of the system operates through dreams. All we can do is behave; we cannot not-behave. Also, the "picture album" is more receptive to concrete representation than to negative command. For example, probably every parent has experienced a child's spilling the milk after being told, "Don't spill the milk." A baseball coach who tells the player, "Don't strike out! Don't make an error!" will quickly observe a strikeout or an error. Consequently, the plan must be what Ford (1977) calls a Do-plan, a positive plan of action.

Dependent on the Doer

A plan dependent on the doer is one that the client can do independently of what others do. In group counseling sessions at a halfway house for women ex-offenders, I encountered residents who said they would look for a job at 8:00 A.M. if the staff would wake them early enough. Such a plan seems doomed to failure, even if the staff were so inept as actually to allow such a practice to take place. Plans that are conditional upon the behavior of others result in clients' giving the power to others which should be their own. This type of planning results in clients' feeling that they are not the captains of their own ships, but only passengers at the mercy of others. The therapist must listen for words and phrases that I refer to as "escape hatches to failure." They allow clients to escape to weaknesses or ineffective behaviors—giving up, negative symptoms, or even addictions—and to lack of control over their lives while still maintaining an illusion of strength and control. Phrases such as, "I'll try," "I'll do it if," "I might," "I could," "Probably . . ." allow for the possibility (or even the probability) of failure and yet provide a false face-saving device (pun intended!). The client can justify failure: "I would have gotten up to look for a job, but the staff didn't wake me." In other words, the failure is not the client's, but someone else's. The best responses to these escape hatches are: "I know you'll try, but will you do it?" "Might? Does that mean yes or no?" "I know you can, but *will* you do it?" "Probably? Will you make a decision either to do it or not to do it?"

The counselor focuses on the *client* rather than on the world external to the client, which is beyond control. This focus is not easy, as the client often resists, especially in disciplinary cases, when being pressured to receive counseling, when exhibiting angering behaviors, and many other times. Yet we all have control *only* over our own world of wants ("picture albums"), our behavioral and perceptual systems. Gaining more effective control over these elements occurs only with effort and hard work.

Specific

A specific plan is concrete and exact. One of the most powerful questions in the therapist's repertoire is, "When?" Many clients express that, "Someday I'll do it" or "I think I'll . . ." or "I'd like to . . ." The experienced Reality Therapist is capable of skillful questioning and is adept at timing. Using words sparingly is helpful, and a simple, well-timed "When?" can be critical. To make the plan specific and concrete, additional questions such as "What?" "Where?" "With whom?" "How often?" need to be answered. The dialogue at the end of the section on planning will illustrate this and other qualities of effective planning.

Repetitive

A repetitive plan is one that is performed repeatedly, if not daily. To overcome the negative symptoms of acting out, depressing, psychosing, negative thinking, psychosomatic aches and pains, and so on, it is necessary to replace them with positive symptoms. The positive symptoms described in Chapter 10 are constructive actions—positive feelings of joy, trust, and the like; rational and positive thinking; and healthful activities such as diet, exercise, personal hygiene, and so on.

The Replacement Program, which is a personal growth agenda, consists of substituting positive symptoms for negative ones, and is accomplished only through repetitive planning. An athlete does not attain top physical condition by exercising when "the spirit moves him", be that once a week, once a month, once a year. Likewise, a person develops positive symptoms and positive addictions by repeated, continuous, and repetitive planning, planning, and more planning!

Applegate (1979) states that repetitive plans must be formulated every day to build strength and encourage a client to take charge of his or her life. Most important among his excellent suggestions are the following four points.

1. *Choose every day to approach others first.* This first step might be preceded by the client's simply observing how people relate to each other. Thus clients are often asked to go to a shopping center or an airport, and observe people talking, greeting each other, saying good-bye, and so on. These plans are best written down, then discussed in detail in subsequent counseling sessions. Plans are then made to greet people, to call them, to smile, and the like.

2. *Choose to achieve something every day.*   Many persons, even those characterized by strength, success, inner control, and flexibility, have moments, hours, days, or even weeks during which their sense of achievement is frustrated. Even high-level business managers realize that the Pareto principle operates in their lives. Also called the 80–20 principle, this rule encompasses many ideas, among them that only 20 percent of a manager's time is controllable. The remaining 80 percent is not within his or her power, in the sense that a manager cannot freely schedule that time. And so, often, the feeling of achievement and control is lessened.

Every parent, child, student, or worker at any level has experienced times of little or no achievement or power. It is useful, indeed crucial, to make specific, attainable, need-fulfilling plans to achieve something each day. The number of plans and their degree of simplicity depend on an individual's strength and control and the amount of time that is realistically controllable. One of the plans that I often suggest to some clients is that they take a brisk walk for fifteen to twenty minutes each day. They can feel that they are doing something healthful and positive. The action is realistic, in that it can be done alone or with someone else and that it costs no money. It is now known that such activities release the endorphins into our system, which cause positive feelings. Consequently, there is scientific basis to the statement of the Danish theologian Soren Kierkegaard: "There is no problem too great that it cannot be solved by walking."

For others, the plans take hundreds of different forms. These achievement-oriented actions are based on work done by the client and the counselor in the process of Reality Therapy. Specific plans are related to the client's wants, current Doing behaviors, and value judgments about what will be effective in providing a sense of achievement or power.

3. *Choose to have fun.*   If the previous two points are related to belonging and accomplishment (self-worth and power), having fun is even more need-fulfilling, in that the client clearly chooses to tell a joke, to read a humorous story, to smile at people, even to watch a funny TV show. For depressing people,

this can be a Herculean task; nevertheless, it's a choice that helps to get them in motion, for "motion goes with positive emotion." And lack of motion usually goes along with apathy, powerlessness, and immobility (depression). In these instances, it is crucial that even a "trivial" plan to have fun be implemented. At the other extreme are workaholics who get high on work, but who have problems in other aspects of their lives. Such hard-driving persons can benefit from fun. However, these "successful" people feel that short-range, simple plans to have fun are a waste of time and won't help. Their desire for grandiosity is transferred from the work setting to the counseling setting. Just as work requires elaborate, grandiose, all-absorbing behaviors, so too the solution to the pain must involve elaborate, grandiose solutions. Even more, then, should the wheeler-dealer make down-to-earth, simple, *repetitive* plans to have fun *each day*.

4. *Choose to act independently.*   In my counseling I emphasize this method of taking charge of one's life. This suggestion is an effort to develop plan-making questions relating to the fourth need: freedom or independence. I ask clients if they can make plans to do something for themselves, either alone or with someone else. The parent, distraught and upset about the behavior of a child, can benefit from independent action chosen to benefit only him- or herself: getting out for an evening, saying no to demands made by other people, and so on. Similarly, some family members are so involved in taking care of an incurably ill person that they give little energy to satisfying themselves or acting independently *for* themselves. Plans to act independently can be immensely useful in helping them fulfill their own needs.

Reality Therapy is thus distinguished from problem solving. Problem solving consists of identifying a problem, brainstorming solutions, and implementing the most desirable one. In some instances, this approach is needed and is very valuable. If a person is not working but has the desire to work and is capable of obtaining a job, it is helpful to work out plans to apply for jobs. On the other hand, if an unemployed client is also depressing and lonelinessing, it is useful to engage in strength-building and more effective control-taking activities such as talking to people, doing a project around the house, getting exercise, reaching out to others in a myriad of ways which can be made more specific in the counseling.

Immediate

Simply stated, the immediate plan is done today or soon. A good question to ask clients is, "What will you do *tonight* to change your life? to have fun? to get along better? to get what you want?" There is a powerful message: "You can change your life for the better . . . and you can do it today!"

Realistic

The attainability of a plan is worked out with the client. Both therapist and client can assess whether the plan is realistic. A slogan summarizing this quality of an effective plan is, "Don't underestimate the value of the minute." Even short-range plans are valuable if the client is enabled to start taking better control. Even successful people sometimes procrastinate. To make a plan and follow through to accomplishment—even to finish one item on a list of ten—brings an emotional payoff, a sense of achievement and pride which nearly everyone has experienced at times.

For the weak client, very short range plans, even plans to do something only once, are helpful. Our angry, upset teenager might be able to say only one friendly statement to a parent. Even though it is not repetitive, still it could be a beginning; "A journey of a thousand miles must begin with a single step," (Lao-Tzu). Again, "Well begun is half done," (Aristotle).

On the other hand, a strong, flexible person can often formulate and implement more detailed, extensive plans. Plans, therefore, are highly individualized and tailor-made for and by the clients, none of whom have exactly the identical amount of strength or control over their present lives.

Process-Centered

A process-centered plan focuses on the action the client can realistically accomplish apart from any ultimate result. This characteristic is similar to several of those just mentioned but includes a slight variation. Below are some examples of process- and outcome-centered plans:

PROCESS-CENTERED PLANS	OUTCOME- OR GOAL-CENTERED PLANS
1. To pay my spouse three compliments.	1. To get along better with my spouse.
2. To take a brisk walk for twenty minutes.	2. To overcome my depression.
3. To meet one new person each day.	3. To form one new friendship.
4. To bowl three times this week.	4. To increase my bowling score by ten points.
5. To eat cereal instead of donuts for breakfast.	5. To lose twenty pounds.
6. To attend the meeting and volunteer one time.	6. To be accepted by a group.
7. To dial the phone.	7. To talk to a friend on the phone.
8. To take a vacation.	8. To relax on vacation.

Process-centered plans are realistic, attainable, dependent only on the person making the plan. Outcome- or goal-centered plans are attained only as by-products of process-centered plans. Yet goals are very important. As stated in Chapter 1, people are more likely to function in a healthful manner if they have identified their wants (goals) clearly and precisely. Nevertheless, goals and outcomes belong in the "picture album" as fundamental wants. The plans comprise the delivery system for attaining those wants and goals.

Following is a listing of several plans. For practice, decide whether they are process-centered or outcome-centered:

1. To be happy.
2. To buy a new car.
3. To be a millionaire.
4. To save $1,000 in exactly a year.
5. To get a job within the next thirty days.
6. To look for a job.
7. To apply for a job at 3 places today.

The value of deciding whether these plans are process- or outcome-centered is in the thinking or discussing, rather than in attaining correct answers. Hence no correct answers are provided; there is no outcome to this brief thinking or discussing exercise, only process.

In summary, the skillful practitioner of Reality Therapy helps clients reverse their thinking and planning—from outcome- to process-centered. This is accomplished both by questioning and by direct, well-timed teaching.

Evaluated

Before the plan is carried out, it should be examined with the client. Does it fulfill the criteria for an effective plan? Is it repetitive, realistic, attainable, and so on? Also, every plan should relate to the client's needs and wants. This linkage is affected through the skillful questioning of the therapist; for example, "What want and need does the plan fulfill?" This is obviously most helpful after the client has been taught that all behavior is designed to fulfill needs and wants.

Of course, not every plan made in counseling can fulfill *all* the criteria. A therapist need not feel obligated to help the client formulate a perfect plan every time. The characteristics discussed in this chapter constitute an ideal, a target. Nevertheless, an effective plan is—at least—specific, attainable, and immediate. Moreover, the plan should be evaluated again *after* its execution. In a subsequent meeting, both client and therapist should review the implementation of the plan: When was it successful? How was it lacking? Where did it break down? Was it carried out as planned? Does it need to be changed? How? Should it be increased in any way?

Firm

This quality of a plan is a transition to the commitment procedure. The client is asked to write the plan down, or to repeat it. The therapist provides reinforcement that it is a good plan, and that it can be a big step toward fulfilling wants, toward mental health. Even if the plan seems small, easy, and trifling, the therapist reminds the client that, "inch by inch anything is a cinch" and that the way to eat an elephant is "one bite at a time."

Reinforced

Finally, the plan is reinforced after its completion. This obviously occurs in subsequent sessions. Since recognition is a basic human need, it is important that counselors comment, when it is appropriate and helpful, on the successful implementation of a plan.

In concluding this discussion, it is crucial to understand that the twelve characteristics of an effective plan constitute the "perfect" plan. It is rare, however, that a perfect plan is formulated. Rare is the golfer whose score is par for every course. Rare is the ballplayer who bats 1000. Rare is the salesperson who makes a sale with every customer! Effective counselors aim at lofty targets, but most often settle for less than an ideal accomplishment. Counseling, like politics, is "the art of the possible."

Returning to our resenting, angering teenager, the following dialogue might occur. It incorporates the earlier procedures and culminates with the planning procedure, which is woven into the session.

TH: You've told me that yelling, sulking, cursing has not helped you to get along with your parents. Right? [Evaluation]

CL: Yeah.

TH: What about avoiding them and not talking? [Evaluation]

CL: It hasn't worked either.

TH: What about seeing them as enemies? [Evaluation]

CL: Nope!

TH: Did you study for your classes in the last week? [Behavior]

CL: Nope!

TH: What do you think about not studying? [Perception and Evaluation]

CL: I'm gonna flunk.

TH: Do you want to pass? [Wants]

CL: Of course!

TH: Do you see a relationship between grades and studying? I admit this is a rather basic question! [Perception and Evaluation]

CL: Yeah! I know. I'm bringing on the poor grades myself!

TH: No, maybe the teachers are out to get you! [Paradoxical statement]
How do you see it? [Perception]

CL: They sure are pickin' on me.

TH: Do you want to change the situation? [Wants]

CL: I don't want to flunk the year.

TH: Do you want to feel better about school, pass the course, get along with the teachers, have a better home life? Or do you want to continue to make your life miserable? [Wants]

CL: I hate the way things are!

TH: Do you want to turn your life around? [Wants]

CL: I do!

TH: What could you choose to do tonight to do that? [Planning]

CL: If my old man yells at . . .

TH: [Interrupting] What will you *choose* to do tonight for yourself? [Planning]

CL: I could be friendly. That's what I'll do . . . I'll be friendly from now on. . . . A nice sweet kid.

TH: Is that possible to be perfect forever? [Evaluation]

CL: [hesitation]

TH: What would you commit yourself to for the rest of the week . . . 'till Saturday? [Planning]

69

CL: I'll be good.

TH: How? [Planning]

CL: I won't argue or fight.

TH: What *will* you do? [Planning]

CL: I'll smile at them.

TH: How often? [Planning]

CL: All evening?

TH: How about just a few smiles? [Planning]

CL: You want me to tell you exactly how many times I'm going to smile tonight at my parents?!

TH: Yep! [All Procedures]

CL: Four times.

TH: When? [Planning]

CL: When I feel like it.

TH: When will you feel like it? [Planning]

CL: You want to know the exact times?

TH: Yep! [All Procedures]

CL: When I come home from school.

TH: When is that? [Behavior]

CL: At quarter after four.

TH: Will you smile at your mother when you walk in the door tonight? [Planning]

CL: Yes, I said I would!

TH: What time? [Planning]

CL: Quarter after four this afternoon.

TH: Could you practice it for me now? [Planning]

CL: I could.

TH: Would you? [Planning]

CL: [Smiles] How's that?

TH: Fair. Try it again. [Planning]

CL: [Smiles broadly] Better?

TH: Fantastic! One more thing. . . . What could you think about at that moment that would help you smile? [Perception and Planning]

CL: I dunno.

TH: You have a job. Right? [Behavior]

CL: Yes.

TH: You want more money! Right? [Wants]

CL: Right.
TH: How about imagining that your mother got a call from your boss and your salary is doubled? If she told you this, would you be able to give her a big smile? [Planning]
CL: I sure could!
TH: Do you see the point I'm making? [Perception]
CL: Yeah! If I think of something I want a lot, I'll smile better!
TH: You're absolutely right. What about the rest of the week? [Perception]
CL: What about it?
TH: Would you greet your mother like that every night till Saturday? [Planning]
CL: I could.
TH: Will you? [Planning]
CL: Yes, I will.
TH: Once again, give me the smile. [Planning]
CL: [Smiles broadly]
TH: How about a firm handshake on it? [Commitment]
CL: [Shakes therapist's hand firmly; Commitment]

In this dialogue, the therapist helps the client make a plan that fulfills most of the characteristics for an effective plan. There are many other plans that could have been formulated. The purpose here is not to describe the best possible plan available, but rather to demonstrate plan making as a procedure in Reality Therapy. The procedures are combined to illustrate how they are not practiced in lockstep fashion. Rather, they are interwoven in an artful way so as to gradually proceed to the commitment phase.

The exploration of behavior, the evaluation, and the planning phases of Reality Therapy are often called the Responsibility Steps. In examining current Doing behaviors, in evaluating wants as well as the effectiveness of efforts to fulfill wants, and in making plans, clients learn that they are already in charge of their lives to some extent. Even more, they realize that the solutions to problems are, as Shakespeare says, "not in our stars, but in ourselves. . . ." They become aware that happiness depends not on how they are treated by the external world, but on the choices they themselves make. They learn, "It's not the force of the gale, but the set of the sail that shows you the way to go." This was summarized by a client who recently said to me, "I guess I have to stop waiting for things to happen and start to make something happen."

Commitment to the Plan

This procedure is an extension of the planning phase. In eliciting a commitment, the client is asked to write down the plan, to fill out a planning sheet, to call or stop back, to tell someone else about the plan, or to shake hands. There are many ways to express commitment. Essentially, it means putting a seal on the plan, "signing the contract," "closing the deal", and so on. Questions like the following are useful: "Are you *really* going to do it?" "Now, would you repeat what you are going to do?" "Would you sign the paper stating that you'll follow through on it?" Rehearsing the plan can be a form of commitment, thus the counselor in the above dialogue asked the difficult teenager to rehearse the smile. Discussing and evaluating consequences can help elicit a commitment, and many useful questions can be formulated such as, "What will be the consequences if you change your mind or don't follow through on the plan?" Thus commitment often includes a discussion of consequences. (I once asked a client to donate $5 to a political candidate he disagreed with for each time he did not follow through on his plans!)

One Final Word about the Procedures

The process of Reality Therapy has been formulated in easily understood vocabulary. There is little jargon or esoteric phraseology. This formulation, nevertheless, represents a fundamental philosophical point about human existence. The fact that, as human beings, we can alter our destinies and take charge of the way we live our lives is by no means shallow or superficial. It is a profound principle, for instance, that we can be happy, fulfilled, and more in control of our feelings and our lives by taking action, by making plans. It is by no means a philosophy that is universally accepted. Yet Reality Therapists believe the words of William James, the father of American psychology, who said, "We do not sing because we are happy. We are happy because we sing." And as William Glasser says, "we are always happy when we choose to sing."

* 7 *

Using Paradoxical Techniques

> **Paradox**   *A tenet contrary to received opinion; also, an assertion or sentiment seemingly contradictory, or opposed to common sense, but that yet may be true in fact.*
>
> —*Webster's New Collegiate Dictionary*

Before reading this chapter, there is an exercise you should perform. Close your eyes and try to *force* them open. It is difficult if not impossible to force your eyes open. Now close them again and simply *allow* them to open. How easy it is! You have just experienced a paradox. Sometimes it is easier to accomplish a task or achieve a goal in a paradoxical way than it is to complete it in a direct way. (Weeks 1982)

Many Reality Therapists have often helped clients make plans only to have them report, "I didn't do it" or, "It didn't help me." The conventional method of practicing Reality Therapy is to repeat the efforts to help them make plans. Yet a closer look at the theory and practice of the method indicates that there are many more subtle ways to accomplish behavior change.

After years of observing Dr. Glasser teach, as well as my own practice of Reality Therapy, I have found it useful to include in the guidelines the admonition, Do the Unexpected. When the client expects an argument, don't argue. If the client anticipates a discussion of inflexible behavior, stress strength-inducing, in-control behavior. (This useful tool should be used only occasionally.)

Examples of Paradox

In a training tape (see Bibliography) in which Dr. Glasser and Fitz-George Peters role-play, Glasser (1976) seeks to put as much distance as possible between himself and the irresponsible behavior of Fitz-George, the client. Instead of saying that he understands the problems of the ex-offender, he states the opposite. He doesn't even drink coffee, much less take drugs. Fitz-George replies, "How can you help me if you don't even drink coffee?" The ingenious reply is that Glasser's job is not to help him be irresponsible; he can do that on his own. (Later Glasser states that his job is to help Fitz-George find a job, and so on.) Glasser's apparent effort to put distance between himself and the client has a reverse effect. It *increases* the involvement or friendship. This use of paradox is a theme in much of Glasser's teaching. When a hypochondriac woman repeatedly tells him that no physician has found anything wrong, Glasser (1976) unexpectedly replies, "My God, you're sick. There's not a part of you that's well." She is caught off guard and later states that she finally experiences some hope of recovery. Paradoxically, she feels a surge of hope when someone finally admits there is something wrong with her.

In a role-play in Columbus, Ohio, before five hundred people, Glasser (Wubbolding, *Dr. William Glasser,* 1982) helped a "client" deal with his obsessing thoughts about religion. Instead of doing the expected—that is, helping the "client" make a plan to do something to overcome them, to keep busy, and so on— Glasser suggested that he simply accept the obsessing thoughts and say to himself, "Okay, I'm going to have these thoughts for a few minutes." In other words, he is to "choose" the symptom rather than fight it.

In my supervision of a Reality Therapy trainee who was unsuccessfully trying to overcome nervousing feelings about her certification program, I prescribed that she spend five minutes a day imagining the following: She is at the Marina Del Rey Hotel, where the final "test" is being conducted. She is in a group of trainees and she makes a complete fool of herself. She does everything wrong. She sees the other trainees ridiculing her! I added that she should try to feel as nervous as she can. One week later, the trainee stated that, "the more I did this, the less I was able to feel upset."

Role-playing seems to lend itself to the effective teaching of paradox. In a consultation session with a counselor at a drug program, I illustrated the use of paradox with a "client" who had run away several times. Upon returning after these journeys, the "client" felt she wanted to put the past behind her and go forward. She said that this time she felt confident. She had hit bottom and learned her lesson. (She knew the conventional application of Reality Therapy!) I asked her if she had previously tried this approach of putting the past "behind" her. She hesitatingly answered yes. I asked, "Has putting it behind you worked?" She answered, "No . . . and because of that I'm a little shaky." I told her that I'd like to see her adopt the nickname "Shaky," and tell everybody in the program about her name. She should act shaky—exaggerate it, pretend to be even shakier than she really is. In other words, she should choose "shakiness" instead of pretending it doesn't exist. After all, her choice of self-confidencing behaviors was not only shallow, it simply had not worked.

A final example of doing the unexpected illustrates how, in some instances, it is quite simple and can provide new learning for participants. In teaching a management workshop, I congratulated a supervisee (in role-play) for being on time for work two times, even though she had been late three times. This seemed rather simple and basic to me as leader. But for at least one of the participants, this comment was amazingly unexpected. He stated, "You blew me away when you congratulated her."

These examples show that doing the unexpected or using paradox can be subtle or simple—or, stated paradoxically, "subtly simple." Only a few of the many types of paradox are cited here, but the theory and practice of Reality Therapy lend themselves to its extensive use. Following are some of the paradoxes in the underlying theory and practice of Reality Therapy, as well as the paradoxical techniques of reframing and prescriptions, including paradoxical intention. This is followed by guidelines and contraindications for their use.

Paradoxes in the Theory of Reality Therapy

To perceive paradox in Reality Therapy, or in life in general, it is necessary to think paradoxically. And thinking paradoxically about Reality Therapy means looking at it in a different light. Therefore, the ideas described below are not new ideas. Rather, they are the fundamental principles of Reality Therapy seen from a different point of view. This different perception is new.

Learning Reality Therapy

When people learn Reality Therapy, especially the Cycle of Counseling, for the first time, they often comment that the ideas are easy to understand. Upon putting them into practice, however, they discover quickly that it is a difficult method to practice. The jargon-free ideas are "deceptively simple." They are easy to understand and hard to do. And with the recent development and refinement of the underlying principles (Glasser 1985) this paradox is even more evident. Though the ideas might seem easy at first glance, nevertheless, as Glasser has frequently stated, it takes approximately two years to see the world through the window of Reality Therapy and its underlying Control Theory.

Fulfillment of Needs

The most basic human drive is to fulfill needs (Glasser 1981, 1986). Yet these needs cannot be fulfilled directly. They can be met only through another mechanism: the "picture album" of specific wants. A further paradox is that the wants can be achieved only in the external world, yet we are part of that world and so some of the needs are fulfilled inside ourselves. Furthermore, this external world is the most difficult of all components to change. Even though human behavior is purposeful—designed to mold the external world—yet this external world is very "unmoldable" (uncontrollable). Many persons seek counseling in order to learn new ways to change another person—a spouse, a teacher, a child, and so on. But anyone who has tried to change another person can testify to the difficulty of such an effort.

Conflict in Need Fulfillment

The fulfillment of one need is both liberating and confining. Even though needs overlap, at times they are in conflict with one another. For instance, fulfilling the need for power or achievement is sometimes tantamount to not fulfilling the need for fun. Even Reality Therapists take work home with them and thus occasionally miss an opportunity to have fun! Similarly, selecting one picture to fulfill human need(s) implies not selecting another. This is similar to Pascal's Circle of Knowledge: "The greater the circle of knowledge, the larger the perimeter of ignorance." Straus (1982) states, "Every choice you make, everything you do is a kind of cage. It is a cage because by doing this you are choosing that you can't be doing something else. Every action you take excludes a range of alternative possibilities."

Behavioral System

The paradox just described occurs when the "picture album" and the behavioral system overlap. But in the behavioral system alone there are several paradoxes and counter-paradoxes. First, the element in the behavioral system that receives most attention in the practice of Reality Therapy is the Doing, or Acting, component. Yet as we live our daily lives, we are more aware of the other two components, Feeling and Thinking. An experience common to many people is that of driving a car after having received some frustration-producing news—loss of a job, death of a relative, a "Dear John" letter, and the like. Awareness of the Doing component—driving the car—might be minimal. On the other hand, awareness of feelings—depressing, angering, being rejected, and so on—are very prominent. Consequently, it is not unknown for accidents to occur; people say, "My mind was a million miles away," or, "I wasn't watching what I was doing."

A further paradox is that in Reality Therapy we *do deal with feelings,* but not by talking exclusively about them, "getting in touch with them," "locating them," "ventilating them," and so on and so on. "Talking about" and "dealing with" are not identical. To talk about feelings of hunger is to deal with them very ineffectively. To talk endlessly about depressing, angering, resenting, self-pitying, and so on is to fail to get to the root of the problem in the behavioral system—the Doing component. Thus the admonition for the Reality Therapist is, "change the Doing component." In counseling a person who is depressing, the Reality Therapist does the unexpected. Instead of talking about the depression, the focus is on giving the component of the behavior which has received the least attention in the life of the depresser—the Doing component. The client is asked to describe a specific day in detail, in order to focus the person's perception on the Doing component.

In some cases the paradox of stressing the Doing component is very ineffective. Many therapists have experienced the individual, couple, or family who repeatedly makes plans and fails to execute them. The process of planning to do something is not working. The therapist can often help the client achieve the same goal by stressing the Thinking component and the "picture album." In other words, "if planning isn't working, stop planning." Paradoxically, the goal can often be achieved by utilizing the Thinking component combined with the "picture album." First, the desired event is implanted in the "picture album" as a want and then the client is instructed to visualize it as present in his or her life. Maltz (1960) cites a research study that showed only a tiny difference in accuracy between those basketball players who practiced shooting free throws for twenty minutes a day and those who spent twenty minutes a day visualizing themselves as successful free-throw shooters. Therefore, utilizing the "imagination" of Maltz (the "picture album" and the Thinking component), the subjects were able to achieve their goals and attain their wants in the external world. In my own life, I used this method to establish a counseling and training center. I announced to some friends that, three years from a given date, I would open such a center. I followed the advice of Maltz, and did not concern myself with how to achieve it. To stress the Doing component would have resulted in discouraging behaviors. Instead, I posted the date on the mirror and looked at it at least each morning and evening. Ten months later the center opened for business. Needless to say, I utilized this form of paradox in my own counseling. In the words of Emerson, "Beware of what you want. In all likelihood you will get it."

In Reality Therapy the purpose of all behavior is to mold the external world to match inner pictures or wants. When clients seek counseling, they do so because their behavior is ineffective in molding that world and thus they are in pain. They sometimes want the therapist to help them find a new way to control, or mold, the world. Ironically, it is this precise goal that is most difficult to achieve directly, for it is almost impossible to change the external world. Applegate (1980) summarizes this difficulty in the title of his chapter in *What Are You Doing?* (Glasser 1980): "If Only My Spouse Would Change." The paradox occurs when clients change their wants or their own behavioral systems; paradoxically, their external world often subsequently changes. When parents of an incorrigible teenager learn to stop criticizing the child, they are often pleasantly surprised to find that the child's behavior changes subsequent to their own behavioral change. On the other hand, the more the parents push, the greater is the resistance. The analogy of forcing your eyes open illustrates the difference between trying to force a change or allowing a change to occur. In attempting to change only those elements over which the client has control, a paradox often occurs; there is also a change in the environment.

The Process of Reality Therapy

There are several paradoxes in the use of Reality Therapy that relate to the overall counseling process rather than to the theory. The most obvious is that progress in gaining better control is made easier and quicker if several fronts are attacked simultaneously in an unexpected way. Thus, an overweight person con-

80

sumed with dieting, food, and losing weight can effectively work on several fronts at the same time. (It is important to emphasize that these several fronts are not the surface, or presenting, problems.) To develop a self-improvement reading program, keep a log, practice being assertive, approach other people, and take brisk walks are ways for the client to take better control and to replace negative symptoms with positive ones. Replacing lack of control, or weakness, with effective control, or strength, is a total effort. Gaining strength and solving the all-consuming problem of weight occur simultaneously.

The cause of a problem is often the effect and vice versa. After several sessions, Scot, a client of mine who was depressing and doing only the minimal amount of work on his job, decided that his depressing was the *result* of not working at his job, not the *cause* of poor performance, as he had originally suspected. Scot was also worried about his use of time and, in fact, was troubled by a philosophical question as to how to control time itself. The result was that he made very little effective use of time, felt it was slipping away from him, and loafed on the job, guilting and depressing himself with a great deal of pain. Again, the effect was the cause, not vice versa. A Reality Therapist using paradox looks at a client's behavior in an unconventional, inverse way, seeing the cause of a situation as the effect and vice versa.

Fundamental to Control Theory is that people want to control their perceptions. We are in control when we perceive ourselves as adequate, popular, successful, rich, tolerant, accepted, and so on. But simply wanting such a perception is not sufficient for attaining it. We attain the perceptions we want by generating total behavior. It is possible but very difficult to directly change a perception—for example, to see someone as good instead of bad. Changes in perception usually occur through changes in behavior. Thus, adjusting a client's perception from a high to a low level—for example, changing a person's perception of a salary from that of "an unacceptably low salary" to simply "a salary," without making judgments—is difficult to accomplish through a single decision. If it is to be accomplished at all, the change will probably be through a change in behaviors geared to a lower level parallel to a low level of perception (see Chapter 1, Principle 5). Similarly, if a person treats a disliked associate in a friendly way, it is often possible to perceive that person more favorably. The change in perception is started by a change in behavior.

In his teaching of Reality Therapy, Dr. Richard Hawes, a faculty member of the Institute for Reality Therapy, is fond of saying, "Don't take the problem too seriously." It is often very helpful to have fun with a person who has a "heavy" problem. Ridiculing is not appropriate, but helping the client realize that the problem is treatable and that there is hope can be accomplished with some lightheartedness.

A less obvious example of paradox in the Reality Therapy process is in the use of questions. One of the functions of the Reality Therapist is to teach clients a better way to live. This is rarely done by lectures, but by skillful questioning. In using appropriate questions the therapist sends an implicit message: "You have power over your life. You can change. A better life is possible." In asking, "Is what you're doing helping?" there is the message that a better course of action is possible. In asking, "What do you plan to do tonight to change your life?" there is the message that an immediate course of action will help the person take charge of his or her life. In asking, "What do you want?" there are many messages: that the person is an important person and that his or her desires are important; that he or she can get at least part of what is wanted, and so on. By asking questions, the counselor enters the client's world, but also attempts to aid the person to learn and to change his or her Thinking behavior as it relates to the very content of the counseling. Clients begin to change their thinking from, "This is an overwhelming problem" to "I believe I can handle it."

In summary, both the theory and the practice of Reality Therapy contain many paradoxes. It is helpful to view them in a new light in order to incorporate paradoxical procedures. Therefore, the ideas just discussed shed a different light on the same material so that new aspects emerge.

Paradoxical Techniques

For purposes of simplicity, the techniques of paradox are divided into two general types: (1) reframing (relabeling or redefining) and (2) prescriptions.

82

Reframing (Relabeling and Redefining)

This technique consists of helping clients change the ways they think about a topic. What was once seen as bad is now seen as good; the problem thus becomes more desirable. In counseling a young man whose hand was "frozen" into a fist (with no physiological basis), I once suggested that he hold it up for all to see rather than hide it under his other arm, as was his habit. We both laughed and were able to see humor in what had been only a "serious" problem for him. I suggested that he try to feel proud of his temporary handicap, and that if he hid it no one would know when he overcame it. I asked, "Why not use it to show people you can conquer difficulties?" He was able to reframe the problem in a twofold manner: from seriousness to humor; and from a shameful event to a positive, attention-getting tool. Reframing, or relabeling, is especially useful in Reality Therapy. To ask what someone is "choosing" to do is to reframe the Doing behavior and help him or her think more in the context of Reality Therapy, rather than in a stimulus-response mentality wherein the person lays responsibility on other people or on external events. In this latter way, many clients ascribe power over their lives to forces outside themselves through such thinking as, "That person upsets me," "I'm depressed because I'm unemployed," "My job is stressful," and so on. So there is a powerful message implicit in such questions as, "What are you *choosing* to do?" Weeks and L'Abate (1982) suggest congratulating a family that seeks help in counseling so that, whereas previously they felt failure, they can now reframe this thinking to recognize that only a family with strength and which cares about each other can admit to the need for help. In Reality Therapy this same technique is used with individuals as well.

Another example is that of relabeling the negative symptom —for example, helping the depressing person see the depression as a friend. The depression becomes a personal friend who accompanies the client, and can be discussed in the third person. Humor can easily be interjected so that the problem (friend) becomes less burdensome. The goal is for the client to think of the depression as a choice rather than as "a cloud that came over

83

me." If this reframing occurs, the "friend" can more easily be dropped in favor of more helpful "friends." (Obviously, a psychotic person should not be encouraged to think along these lines!) Reframing, or relabeling or redefining, is a way to help clients think in new ways about problems. It is most helpful for the therapist to intentionally look for new ways to think about problems presented by clients. Just as effective Reality Therapists help clients discover alternative ways to drive their total behaviors, so also can they help clients discover new ways to view the problems. Following is a list of "labels," similar to that of Weeks (1982), that are generally seen as negative. How many positive "labels" can you find for each of these words?

Aggressive
Passive
Angry
Upset
Backslapping
Withdrawn
Submissive
Looking out for #1
Domineering
Dependent
Controlling
Self-critical
Crying
Oversensitive
Thick-skinned
Self-centered
Whining
Impulsive
Inconsistent
Moody

Prescriptions

In this technique, the symptom is prescribed. That is, the client is told to choose the symptom. Victor Frankl is one of the early writers who described prescriptions. In his logotherapy, he utilized Paradoxical Intention. With certain problems, such as anxiety or phobias, Frankl (1960) encouraged the client "to intend or wish, even if for a second, precisely what he fears." He describes, for example, a young man troubled by excessive sweating. The young man was instructed to tell people how much he sweated and even to brag about it. Frankl reports that, after phobicking for four years, the client was able quickly to overcome the problem permanently. In this case as in others, using humor is important. Frankl (1960) quotes Gordon Allport: "The neurotic who learns to laugh at himself may be on the way to self-management, perhaps to cure." Weeks and L'Abate (1982) add several refinements of prescribing that are useful in Reality Therapy.

Scheduling a Symptom. An upset person schedules the negative feelings. In counseling a young man rejected by his girlfriend, I instructed him to have an "unhappy hour" the next day at 5:00 P.M. He was to indulge his angering, depressing, and self-pitying. He gave himself permission to "crank it up" and indulge it to its fullest. I called him several days later to ask whether he had followed through on his plan. He stated that he was "too busy to take the time to go to 'unhappy hour!' "

Restraining a Behavior. Milton Erickson is known for prescribing resistance. When a client chooses not to change, he or she is warned of the negative consequences of change—the effects on family, friends, self. This is seen as puzzling to the client in view of his or initial resistance to change. The counselor might even state that change is next to impossible. For example, in counseling a man who had been angering for many years, I said, "You'll probably have this anger for a long time, maybe forever." He replied almost angrily, "But I don't want it. I want to get along better at work and at home." I responded, "Are you prepared to fail in your efforts to fight it?" His answer was no. "Then I predict you'll fail even more," was my response. He said, "How will I conquer it?" "By accepting it and failing in your efforts and by accepting your failures." He said nothing further . . . and merely thought about it! I also prescribed long, solitary walks for times when he was not angry. During those walks he was to choose to be as angry as possible. (It is very difficult to generate anger and take a *long,* brisk walk at the same time.)

Prescribing a Relapse. The previous example illustrates the paradoxical technique of encouraging a client to choose the symptom, with another component added: making the choice to relapse very difficult (that is, to anger while walking briskly). An essential component of prescription is that the client is told to choose the symptom, to schedule it, to embrace it as a "friend." The therapist asks him- or herself, "How can I join the resistance?" Whether the paradox is a detailed prescription or a cryptic insightful remark, it should be discussed minimally, without "teaching" the purpose of it. If clients subsequently describe how they defied the plan (the prescription), the counselor should shun any detailed discussion of how the plan was made with the purpose of noncompliance. (Some prescriptions are given by the counselor expecting defiance. The client is thus in a double-bind: to follow through on the plan and to choose the symptom, or to *not* follow through and *not* choose the symptom.) Following are twenty behaviors. As an exercise, list one prescription for each behavior. Keep in mind the need to "join the resistance."

Temper tantruming
Depressing
Adolescent with a messy room and the mother yelling at
    him or her
Husband making unreasonable demands on the wife
Procrastinating
Smoking
Person being unhappy with the spouse's drinking
Wife whose husband oversleeps
Parent of adolescent who steals
Person exhibiting shy behaviors
Person blushing excessively
Person being afraid of passing out during an exam
Family of a father who angers excessively

Worrying

Person "overpreparing" for a test

First-grader thumb-sucking

Single person searching desperately and unsuccessfully for a spouse

Seventh-grade girl refusing to study

Eight-year-old boy keeping every school paper in his schoolbag

Man or woman who is "martyring"

Why Paradoxical Procedures Work

There have been few adequate and comprehensive discussions of why paradoxical procedures are effective. But the principles underlying Reality Therapy provide a clear explanation of their effectiveness. One such principle is that all behavior has a purpose: to control the world to get what we want, or to mold the environment to match our internal pictures (see Chapter 1, Principle 3). If people exaggerate the symptoms or think of them in another way (reframing), the purpose of their phobicking or anxieting is changed. There is less "control" of other people and more control of their own behavior.

When people control others less, the payoff is removed through the conscious choice to perform the behavior. This, indeed, does not make "logical" sense. Rather, it is paradoxical. That is, it must be seen in conjunction with the other side of the coin: they are now in more effective control of the behavior. They gain a more explicit feeling of being in control of their behaviors. If clients attempt to control people or situations by nervousing, sweating, or the like—which obviously is not working or helping—they are told to choose, schedule, or exaggerate those noneffective behaviors. Thus, they learn that controlling the world by these behaviors is not helping. This seems, at first, illogical to them. Yet it is not illogical. It is paradoxical. And one must think paradoxically to see the logic that it results ultimately in more control.

Another principle of Reality Therapy is that most behaviors

87

are chosen (see Chapter 1, Principle 4). When people complain of problems, they feel out of control, as though the problem has hold of them. Reframing and prescriptions help clients to not only *feel* control but also to *see* their behavior as a choice. If a choice can be made to feel more anxious, then a choice can be made to feel less anxious, too.

And so the concepts of purpose and choice, central to Reality Therapy, help explain the effectiveness of paradoxical methods.

Contraindications for Using Paradoxical Interventions

Paradoxical methods should not be used indiscriminately or irresponsibly. There are few absolute rules about using paradox, yet there are conditions and caveats which any counselor should consider. Thus Weeks and L'Abate (1982), stating that there are very few guidelines for when *not* to use paradox, add that, "The techniques are still so new and exciting that therapists have been focusing on successes and not failures." They cite their own experience as the basis for the following contraindications:

1. A person who feels little involvement with the therapist does not benefit from paradoxical intervention.
2. A sociopathic client does not benefit. Weeks and L'Abate state, "Tasks given . . . do not register."
3. Paranoids are not receptive because they are overly suspicious and might become even more suspicious.
4. Paradox should never be used in cases of destructive behavior—for example, homicidal or suicidal behaviors.
5. When there are acute crises—for example, grief reactions, loss of employment—paradox is not appropriate.
6. Paradoxical interventions are used extensively in family therapy. However, West and Zarski (1983)

suggest that anyone using these techniques be trained in systems theory and receive supervision until training has been virtually completed. Even with training, there are instances when paradox should not be used. Fisher et al. (1981) as well as Weeks and L'Abate (1982) warn against using it in families where there is much chaos and confusion. There must be *patterns* of behavior present in the family before effective paradoxical interventions can take place. When adult members are immature or when hostile behavior is expressed, paradox should be avoided. Finally, families that project responsibility onto others are not appropriate subjects for paradox.

Case Examples

Following are descriptions of six cases. Use these to practice making paradoxical statements of a reframing or prescriptive nature. Remember, though, that paradoxical statements should not be made indiscriminately or in a cookbook fashion. They must be well timed and used sparingly.

1. Mike is nervous about his driver's test. The more he practices and studies, the more anxious he gets. He has worked hard to overcome this anxiety, but has had no success.
2. Mrs. Jones is angry at her nineteen-year-old son, who works full time and lives at home with her. He spends money "irresponsibly," keeps very late hours, and eats too much food.
3. Susan and Thomas have a fairly strong marriage but want it to be better. He makes most of the decisions, and she is mostly passive, deferring to him. She occasionally gets depressed. He enjoys bowling.
4. Mr. and Mrs. Brown complain that their fifteen-

year-old son is withdrawn and remote. He won't interact with the other members of the family. He is surly and sarcastic when he does speak. They've tried coaxing, punishing, and bribing him, which haven't helped.

5. Billy blushes. Any time someone mentions his name, he turns red. This creates a social problem for him among his friends. He fights it continually, but nothing works.

6. Mrs. Green complains that her husband has a terrible temper. When he doesn't get his way, he yells and threatens. She in turn fights back, but eventually gives in. She is tired of losing her own temper and also tired of giving in. She wants the situation to change.

* 8 *

Marriage and Family Counseling

The use of Reality Therapy in marriage and family counseling is in its early stages. And so there is no comprehensive model of Reality Therapy applied to marriage and family. This chapter is an attempt to enhance the development of its application, as well as provide an initial, tentative, yet workable way of thinking about marriage and family counseling within the context of Reality Therapy. It would be well to review Chapter 1 at this point to refresh yourself with the principles underlying the process of Reality Therapy.

Reality Therapy and Marriage Counseling

The principles underlying Reality Therapy are clearly applicable to marital relationships. A marriage consists of two human beings who have needs, wants, behavioral systems, and perceptual systems. Consequently, when a marriage endures there is congruence, or overlap, between the members' wants, or "picture albums"; how they live (behave); as well as how they view their world—that is, their values. Conversely, when a marriage or family is not functioning to the satisfaction of its members, there is an incongruence, or lack of commonality, in the

91

members' wants—or "picture albums"—their behavior, or their values. The goal of counseling is to help the members increase the overlap or commonality in the above components, thereby increasing family adjustment, harmony, and happiness.

When a relationship begins between a man and a woman (or between friends), it is because there is immediate congruence in the Feeling components of their behavioral systems. The individuals feel physical and emotional attraction toward each other. This cement binding the relationship in the beginning is merely one aspect of their behavioral systems. If the relationship is to last, there must be added commonality in the components of Doing and Thinking as well as in their wants and values. The couple must do things together. Feelings are not enough to sustain a relationship over a long period of time. Though intense and powerful, feelings are also very changeable, thus they are the weakest force in sustaining a relationship. Over 80 percent of teenage marriages fail not merely because people are "immature," but because the cement binding the "whirlwind romance" could not expand to include commonality in all the components of the both parties' control systems.

Commonality of Wants

All too often a relationship fails when the intensity of the Feeling component cools and the partners investigate the commonality of the other components just described. In deteriorating relationships there is often little overlap between inner "picture albums." One member wants to have a family, the other wants no children. One wants to go to the Baptist Church, the other wants to go to the Roman Catholic Church. One wants friendship with politically liberal people, the other wants friends who vote only for candidates endorsed by the John Birch Society. One wants a quiet life by the fireplace, the other wants an active life of community involvement. A crisis occurs when one or both members discover that they adamantly want the other person to match his or her own pictures and *is unwilling to change this want*. (The crisis is compounded when one person is unwilling to change to match the other's pictures.) For example, when a husband and wife both want the female role to be that of a housewife and housekeeper, there is overlap between their "picture albums." In recent years, however, many women have changed the picture of what they want. After many years of wants revolving around the *"kinder, kirche, kuchen,"* some women have recently pictured themselves with careers out of the home. If the husband is willing to change his picture (want) to match the picture (want) of his wife, there is little or no problem. But if, at this point, both refuse to change their pictures of what they want from the other person, there will be a strain in the relationship because of the declining amount of overlap between "picture albums," or wants.

The need most easily fulfilled in the initial stages of a relationship is that of belonging. As the relationship progresses, there is often conflict over the need for power. The question, so often asked by military people, becomes a source of a power struggle and resulting argument: "Who's in charge here?" In the situation just described, this question becomes, "Who will make the decision about whether I (the wife) will have a career outside the home?"

Commonality of Doing and Thinking

Other binding forces requiring congruence are the Doing and Thinking aspects of total behavior. If persons in a relationship spend time together, the relationship will be strengthened; this is discussed in more detail later. Likewise, in marriage as in business, the enterprise will prosper if the partners agree on basic goals, plans, strategies, and the like. When common goals (which more precisely are in the "picture album," or inner world of wants, and thus are seen as need-fulfilling), plans, and strategies are discussed, clarified, and worked toward, they provide a binding force that can compensate for many of the predictable natural differences between people. If a couple has the goal of saving a set amount of money to put toward a down payment on a house, they will work toward it, plan together, and arrive at specific steps to achieve that goal, thereby drawing themselves closer together. "A family that plans together, stands together." On the other hand, if one member wants continually to buy as many creature comforts as possible, or eat often at expensive restaurants, while the other wants to save for a rainy day, the couple will be torn apart by these diverse Thinking and Doing aspects of their total behaviors.

Commonality of Perceptual Systems

Finally, in strong relationships there is congruence in the way both parties view the world around them (their perceptual systems). As stated in Chapter 1, the perceptual system can be seen from either high or low levels. Seeing the world from a high level of perception means making judgments or placing values on things—that is, seeing people, data, things, and ideas as good or bad, important or unimportant, friendly or threatening, moral or immoral, exciting or depressing, pro-American or anti-American, on your side or against you, agreeable to you or unacceptable to you, affecting you positively or affecting you negatively, fair or unfair, wonderful or disastrous, attractive or distasteful, pleasurable or painful, beautiful or ugly, and many more. In all these perceptions a judgment is made. Viewing people, data, things, or ideas from a low level of perception requires being able to suspend judgment. A strong relationship has commonality in its perceptual systems. Both people see the world from similar viewpoints. They put similar values on people, data, things, and ideas. For example, it seems safe to say that most couples have similar politics. If they vote for opposite parties, chances are they don't put much overall value on politics in their lives. It would be rare for one spouse to perceive the Republican party as so important that full-time dedication is required, while the other spouse perceives the Democratic party at that same level of perception and required dedication. The same is true of lower levels of perception. Both people in a successful marriage are able to withhold judgment on many of the same people, data, things, or

94

Marriage and Family Counseling

ideas. In any list of items, they would agree that some are not important.

For example, the following is a list of items about which a couple could either make judgments (put value) or withhold judgment. As an exercise, put a mark (X) in one column for each item, then ask a friend or spouse to do the same and compare the results.

TOPIC	PUTS A VALUE —EITHER POSITIVE OR NEGATIVE		DOES NOT PUT A VALUE— ITEM IS OF LITTLE CONCERN	
	You	Another	You	Another
Being outside in snowy weather				
Owning a big car				
Having a clean kitchen				
Putting away clothes				
Cleaning the car				
Saving money				
Having sex regularly				
Keeping a full tank of gasoline in the car				
Turning the thermostat down				
Going away for the weekend				

TOPIC	PUTS A VALUE —EITHER POSITIVE OR NEGATIVE		DOES NOT PUT A VALUE— ITEM IS OF LITTLE CONCERN	
	You	Another	You	Another
Having friends over				
Visiting in-laws				
Talking about work				
Getting up early on Saturday morning				

If there is little overlap between your responses, there is reason to believe that there is divergence in your perceptual systems. (The above list should not be perceived as scientifically validated. Yet as a test, my wife Sandie and I found we agreed on eleven of the fourteen items, indicating that there is much commonality between the ways we view the world.)

To make matters more complicated, there can be many kinds of judgments made at a higher perception level. There should be some agreement about these judgments in a strong relationship. For example, my wife and I agree that we both view getting up early on Saturday mornings from a high level of perception, though we disagree on whether it is a positive or negative value. For me, rising early is positive; for her, sleeping late on Saturday morning is very, very positive. Any successful relationship involves people who not only put values on the same things, but also put *similar* values on things.

Finally, it should be noted that there is never complete agreement between any two worlds of wants, behavioral systems, or perceptual systems. Nor should there be. It is differences as well as similarities that make life interesting and exciting. The point is that there should be commonality between the systems, not that they should be identical. Identical systems are impossible and undesirable. A strong relationship is not only the result of commonality, but also of negotiating the differences, resolving power struggles, and arriving at satisfactory—though often imperfect—solutions.

Reality Therapy and Family Counseling

The same principles apply if a family is involved; the components just increase geometrically with each person present. There are many more possibilities involved with just one child in the family. This is why many counselors find that couple counseling is manageable but family counseling is too difficult. No counselor should casually or indiscriminately attempt family counseling. Much thought, preparation, and training should precede such efforts.

The process of Reality Therapy as applied to marriage and family counseling can be divided into three phases: assessment, intervention, and action. There is close interplay between the first two, assessment and intervention, in that they can be simultaneous.

ASSESSMENT

In the assessment phase, the overall task of the counselor is to help the family clarify the degree of congruence among the inner "picture albums," perceptual systems, and behavioral systems. The family members thus evaluate their own strengths and weaknesses. They define their individual wants and their common wants, what they expect from counseling, and so on. They also describe their perceptions—that is, how they see each other, what they like about the family, and so on. They describe what they think is helping and hurting the family, emphasizing what each person is doing that is or is not working, what they argue

97

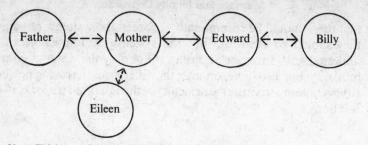

Note: Thickness of lines indicates firmness of alliances.

FIGURE 2: SMITH FAMILY ALLIANCES

about, and how they argue. (In the initial sessions this is done easily by observing the family members interact to determine the existence and amount of quality time spent together, to whom members feel the closest, and so on.)

The latter points are important because the counselor must discover whether and how all members fulfill their needs, especially the power need, within the family. Determining quality time and family alliances points to appropriate intervention in the second phase.

In Figure 2, the alliances of a hypothetical Smith family are illustrated. Mother and Edward are seen as the center of the family. Mother is closely allied with son Edward and less so with Father and daughter Eileen. Billy is somewhat allied with Edward, but is generally on the fringe of the family.

INTERVENTION

After determining the various alliances, it is helpful for the therapist to disrupt them to some extent. This sometimes heightens the anxiety of the family members and gives the illusion that they are getting along with each other even less than they were. Yet it is based on the principle that a family has worked out ways to confront or avoid problems—that is, to handle power struggles. If these ways were working satisfactorily for everyone in the group, there would be no pain felt and they would not be seeking counseling. Alliances are attempts to fulfill wants and needs by resolving conflicts and lessening pain. The counselor's task is to disrupt an ineffective method of resolving problems. The following are two general types of intervention.

Intervention 1

The first intervention in the Smith Family could be to point out how Edward is the center of the family and, in fact, controls other family members. (This would have been determined in the assessment phase.) The counselor might find it helpful to intentionally exaggerate Edward's control in a humorous way. The counselor might also help Father to define whether he wants to be more closely involved with the family—for example, to be more involved with Edward. If Mother is perceived as favoring Edward, the counselor might, paradoxically, suggest that she "favor" him even more, or that when he misbehaves, she take total charge of disciplining him. Edward could be instructed to ask her for favors or to misbehave only in her presence.

These initial interventions are not intended as the only possible ones. They are here to illustrate how Reality Therapy can be applied (especially the evaluation procedure) in a rather subtle and/or paradoxical way to family counseling (see Chapter 7). And so the purposes of intervention are many: to help the more resistant members realize that there is a problem; to teach new ideas; to heighten anxiety; to disrupt alliances; to elicit commitments to the counseling; to help the family increase the congruence among the various "picture albums," behavioral systems, and perceptual systems; and to bring into the open the ever-present power struggles.

Intervention 2

Another appropriate intervention using Reality Therapy is for the counselor to explain how to build strong relationships. Ford (1981) states that there are four steps in building strong relationships. These are also the four methods and levels of intervention

```
┌─────────────────────────────────┐
│          Level A                │
│     Problem Solving:            │
│   Resolving power struggles     │
│   Compromise, Avoiding          │
│   Destructive Arguments         │
└─────────────────────────────────┘
┌───────────────────────────────────────┐
│              Level B                   │
│   Communication, Conversation          │
└───────────────────────────────────────┘
┌─────────────────────────────────────────────┐
│                  Level C                     │
│         Doing Together Alone                 │
│        Strengthening Activities:             │
│     Both parties feel effective control      │
└─────────────────────────────────────────────┘
┌───────────────────────────────────────────────────┐
│                    Level D                         │
│                 Doing Alone                        │
│   Strengthening Activities: Person feels effective control │
└───────────────────────────────────────────────────┘
```

FIGURE 3: METHODS AND LEVELS IN BUILDING RELATIONSHIPS

in marriage and family counseling (see Figure 3). They should
first be applied to groups of two (husband and wife; parent and
one child, and so on), then to the entire family unit. Let's examine each of these levels:

*Level A: Problem Solving—Compromise, Avoiding Destructive
Arguments.* Most people approach a counselor because they
have struggled unsuccessfully for power and have difficulty
compromising. As a result, one person uses arguments as a way
to persuade the other that his or her "picture album," perceptual

system, or behavioral system is better. This is the case with the Smith family. Father attempts to convince Edward that 11:00 P.M. is a reasonable curfew. Edward, not easily convinced, wants to stay out until 3:00 A.M., and does. This is a serious discrepancy between their respective systems, and arguments ensue. Criticisms and accusations are leveled at each other; name calling is thrown in, heightening the anger of everyone. Father reminds Edward, "I've told you time and time again that I want you to hang up your clothes. Why don't you do as I tell you? Your older brother [who has married and left the roost] was never like this. You don't appreciate everything I do for you. I'm not going to tell you again." Edward responds, "What's the difference? It's my room! Why don't you clean up your own mess in the living room? It's a dumb rule. You're picking on me. Billy [the younger brother] gets away with murder. You're a pain in the neck." It is obvious that there is a standoff, a power struggle, an inability to compromise and resolve the power struggle.

Skills needed at this level consist of negotiation. When a struggle or problem is negotiated, all persons get at least part of what they wanted. The goal is to have everyone feel a sense of power and self-worth when the negotiation is completed. This is accomplished when those involved experience three things: (1) they have gotten at least part of what they want, (2) they've been listened to and respected, and (3) the other family members have also moved away from an unbending position. A couple in their fifties who could not agree on whether the wife should resume her professional career after having been ten years away from it came to me for counseling. They continually argued to the point of intense anger. Though they wanted to remain married and had considerable relational strength, the adamant, all-or-nothing posture on the part of both was beginning to strain the relationship. After several sessions, they were able to reach a compromise and resolve the power struggle. The husband, an upper-level manager in a large company, remarked, "I negotiate and compromise every day at work. It never occurred to me to do it at home." (For a more detailed discussion of his compromise, see Chapter 9, the case of a Married Couple.) Similar goals are appropriate for our Smith family.

Level B: Communication, Conversation. Another level of relationship building is that of communication or conversation. People often seek marriage or family counseling because they "can no longer communicate." Parent-child relationships are said to break down because of a "lack of communication." A spouse is said to be unwilling to discuss sex, religion, and so forth. The other person in the relationship often becomes frustrated, angry, resentful, or spiteful. A cold war develops which is characterized by revenge. In the Smith family, Father and Edward not only cannot compromise, but they give little evidence of listening to each other or of trying to enter the other's inner world.

The abilities needed at this level are both listening-questioning skills and assertive-responsible language skills. Listening-questioning skills include asking for opinions from the other person, accepting what is said in a nonjudgmental way, seeking value judgments rather than making them for the other person, clarifying what the other person wants, and many others. Assertive-responsible language skills include a person's telling the other what is wanted or intended, admitting mistakes, and taking responsibility for Feeling and Doing behaviors without blaming others. An effective counselor will teach Father to communicate with Edward and, indeed, with the whole family by such statements as, "Is coming home at 3:00 A.M. against the rules?" or, "I would like you to come home at 11:00 P.M. Are you willing to keep this rule?" "When you stay out till 3:00 A.M., your mother and I worry, and that is not helping us. What do you think about it?" Thus Father learns to communicate in a way that is assertive but not angry, direct but not blameful, and empathetic but not weak.

Levels A and B are used most effectively in relationship building when the lower two levels—Doing Together Alone and Doing Alone—are firmly established. Much contemporary counseling and therapy focuses on family communication and compromise. Yet the harder some couples and families try to communicate and compromise, the more strain they put on their relationships and the more likely they are to resort to power conflicts. The therapist's task, then, is not only to teach effective methods of compromise and communication, but, most important, to assist them with Levels C and D, the foundation for a strong relationship. This is done using the Cycle of Counseling. Thus they are asked to define what they want from each other, to describe in detail their current common total behaviors, to evaluate the effectiveness of these behaviors, and then to plan to do "In Control" or "Strengthening Activities."

Level C: Doing Together Alone—Strengthening Activities. A strong relationship rests on firm building blocks, one of which is characterized by the phrase "Quality Time (QT)." QT consists of time spent exclusively with the other person. During this time, both parties perform a mutually agreed upon activity. For an activity to qualify as QT, it must have several characteristics, the first three of which are closely linked.

1. REQUIRES EFFORT. Activities that are strength building require effort. There must be energy expended.

2. REFLECTS MUTUALLY AGREED UPON VALUES. This is, of course, defined on a very individual basis according to individual perceptual systems.

3. INCLUDES AWARENESS OF THE OTHER PERSON. When activities are strength building, they cannot be done alone or at least not as effectively as when done with another. As Applegate (1980) says, "It is difficult to play tennis alone unless you are very quick." Glasser (1985) emphasizes the need for sharing time and activities if a marriage is to be need-satisfying for both parties.

Stop reading for a moment and think how this level could be applied to our hypothetical Smith family. Then use the following activity list to apply the ideas to your own life. First check those items that you enjoy, then review the list with a partner to determine which activities fulfill the qualities for QT. Add other suitable activities at the bottom in the space provided, if you like.

Activity	You	Your Partner
Going grocery shopping		
Cleaning the garage		
Watching TV		
Going to a party		
Refinishing furniture		
Painting the house		
Planning a vacation		
Yelling at the children		
Taking a brisk walk		
Doing aerobic exercises		
Seeing a movie		
Going camping		
Cooking together		
Planning a menu		
Sleeping		
Having sex		
Visiting friends or relatives		
Taking a class together		
Driving		

Planning a party

_____   _____   _____
_____   _____   _____
_____   _____   _____
_____   _____   _____
_____   _____   _____
_____   _____   _____

When couples or families assess whether they have QT together, they frequently describe the time in terms of three activities that are not strength building: watching TV, driving together, and eating out together. It is a safe prediction that our Smith family spends little time together. They perhaps eat together, go to relatives' homes on holidays, and watch an occasional TV program together. Yet none of these activities builds strength in a relationship very efficiently. In fact, they often provide occasion for increased power struggles. They fail to fulfill at least one of the first three qualities. This is not to say that such activities are *totally* useless in building a relationship, but they do not fulfill the characteristics as well as other activities. For instance, watching TV together is not only an inefficient way to build strong family relationships, but it is in many instances destructive. It can be both the cause of a weak relationship or an escape from a boring, unwanted one. In their excellent book, *The Art of Friendship,* Leefeldt and Callenbach (1980) state the following:

> We cannot leave the subject of obstacles to friendship without mentioning several technological developments which, we believe, have significant but largely unappreciated consequences for our friendship patterns.
>
> Americans spend on the average about five hours a day watching television—more time than they spend on any other waking activity, except work. We find this statistic distressing because in a more relationship-oriented society those five hours would be devoted to family, friends, exercise, education,

or other human-related activities. It is hardly an exaggeration to say that the television set is many Americans' best friend. It gives us our information; it fills up our time; it minds our children; and it relieves us from being active or taking risks that lead to growth. By "killing" time with TV, we prevent those unpredictable, spontaneous happenings that contribute to friendship. If we are glued to the television set, we certainly don't get the idea of going out for a friendly walk. We don't notice that our companion seems to be worried about something or ask what it is, which could lead to an exchange of feelings and mutual support; we don't cope with other people's feelings; we don't get to have interesting arguments; we don't even discuss what is going on in our lives. In short, television is a massive social analgesic balm. The social and personal costs of our national addiction to television watching are incalculable, but friendship is certainly among the chief casualties.

Following are the remaining qualities required if an activity, done together, can accurately be described as QT.

4. PERFORMED REPETITIVELY.   Just as it is necessary to eat and exercise regularly to remain strong and healthy, it is necessary to have QT on a regular basis. Once a week is better than once a month; once a day is better than once a week.

5. PERFORMED FOR A LIMITED AMOUNT OF TIME.   The activity should be done often, but for short periods of time. A daily fifteen-minute walk might be more realistic and attainable for many people than a sixty-minute jog. Doing the dishes together for ten minutes each evening is often more realistic than trying to spend two hours together doing other activities several times per week.

6. SAFE TOPICS ARE DISCUSSED.   There should be no discussion of emotionally charged topics during this period. The conversation should be light. The common topics of interest in the respective systems are the point of focus in the conversation. Therefore, parents who have a "problem child" and whose conversation is generally consumed by discussions about the child, should refrain from mentioning the problem. Similarly, a couple whose relationship is strained should discuss only commonali-

ties. They need to find topics on a low level of perception. If they take a walk together, for example, they can talk about what they see as they walk—neighbors, pleasant memories, funny stories, or events. They must shun all upsetting arguments during those *few* moments. This is extremely difficult to accomplish, for it means lowering the perception level for a few minutes. Clients readily agree to carry out such plans, but find their execution difficult. It should be emphasized that, for some people, intellectual controversy is an effective way to develop strong relationships; discussion of books, current events, and the like often serve to strengthen relationships. Such sessions are appropriate if the parties possess communication skills by which they can convey respect for the other's opinion.

7. NO CRITICISM.   The most important component of QT is an extension of item 6. During the effortful, valuable, limited, repetitive time spent together, there should be positive, constructive talking *without criticism*—that is, without attacks on the other person. When there is strain in a relationship between husband and wife, parent and child, or friend and friend, there is usually criticism. Criticism means one partner's pointing out that the other's "picture album," behavioral system, or perceptual system is inferior. "That opinion is stupid." "You don't know what you're talking about." "You shouldn't do that, think that, or feel that way." These are messages to be avoided during this Quality Time. As Glasser has frequently pointed out in his lectures, "We are all 'picture-album chauvinists,' " yet during the QT all put-downs or even negative comments—no matter how well intentioned—are omitted. The conversation should center on opinions, facts, plans, hopes, goals, other people, and so on. In my counseling, I often paradoxically suggest, "You can always go back to criticizing later. But during this time . . . absolutely no criticism. Now what will you talk about during your QT?"

In marriage and family counseling, as in all Reality Therapy, it is quite acceptable to prescribe a plan of action in the beginning. It is, of course, suggested only after the parties have clearly determined that their current behaviors are not effective and that they want to work on the relationship. One of the best prescriptions for building strength is a brisk fifteen-minute walk every day at a set time. It is very helpful to prescribe that a couple exercise together; such activities are inexpensive, can be done close to home, and require no special preparations. But this suggestion should be recognized as only one activity. There are many plans that can be worked out with clients. As Soren Kierkegaard, the Danish philosopher and theologian, has overstated the point: "There is no problem too great that it cannot be solved by walking."

Let's return to the Smith family. A Reality Therapist would help the members plan to spend Quality Time together. At first it should probably be in pairs: Mother and Father, Father and Billy, Mother and Edward, Edward and Eileen, Father and Edward, Billy and Eileen. This should be done after the family members have made value judgments about their present ineffectual behavior. Perhaps such plans are not even formulated during the first several sessions. But the goal is to help the Smiths stop making endless value judgments about each other, thereby lessening their criticism of each other and allowing them to discover at least some commonality in what they do, think, feel, and want in their family life.

ACTION

There is no clear distinction between the intervention phase and the action phase. The action phase consists of carrying out the plans made in the counseling session. The execution of these plans is best begun during the session. In fact, the plans should have the characteristics of an effective plan as described in Chapter 6; in the beginning of family counseling, however, the plans might not fulfill all the characteristics. The plans could relate to any of the levels of relationships described earlier, especially Level 3.

As stated earlier, the ideas in this chapter represent how Reality Therapy is applied to marriage and family counseling. One such application consists of three phases: assessment, intervention, and action. A major part of these is the utilization of Ford's levels of relationship building, especially Levels A, B, and C. This treatment of Reality Therapy is intended to contribute to the development of a comprehensive model for marriage and family counseling which incorporates these ideas. There are many experts whose marriage and family counseling methods partly fit Reality Therapy—for example, Haley, Minuchin, and Whitaker. You are encouraged to pursue these sources.

* 9 *

Two Cases: A Single Woman and a Married Couple

A Single Woman: Jane

Jane, a forty-three-year-old, overweight, divorced mother of two grown children, came to me with a previous diagnosis of manic-depression. Because of this diagnosis she had been taking various prescribed drugs for fifteen years. Prior to that, she had for years taken many nonprescription drugs. Her life was characterized by a sense of aimlessness wherein she would feel depressed for weeks on end. These feelings of misery would be followed by much shorter periods of excitement. The extremes, however, were not so severe that she was nonfunctional. She held a job for a large company and also worked part time for another company. This gave her some sense of accomplishment and power in her life. She also had two daughters, one of whom lived out of state, but with whom she had a satisfactory relationship. She had a hobby of ceramics, but did not feel that it provided much fun for her. Her life was out of control, in that she felt dependent on the prescription drugs to function, even in her current unsatisfying manner. Her needs were quite unmet, and she suffered many frustrations in her inner "picture album," or world of wants.

We immediately worked hard to define some of her wants. She stated that she wanted to set the following goals related to her needs:

1. To become thin. To lose sixty-five pounds. (Power)
2. To be comfortable around men. (Belonging, Fun, Power)
3. To handle money better. (Power, Self-worth, Freedom)
4. To get to the point where she doesn't need drugs. (Freedom and Power)
5. To keep her house neat. (Power)
6. To eliminate her depression without drugs. (Freedom)

I stated that these wants seemed realistic to me, but that their attainability would depend on "how hard" and "how smart" she would work to achieve them. I further explained that I do not practice medicine and have no advice to give her about medicine, whether it be aspirin or prescription drugs. She should talk over her prescriptions with her physician. (This is an ethical principle that I explain to any client who tells me he or she takes prescription drugs.)

She very quickly examined her own behaviors: how she let her house get very dirty and how she especially had a sense of depression, aimlessness, and loneliness at home in the evening. She decided that doing little at home in the evening was not helping her, and that other plans would be possible. So I repeatedly helped her make value judgments, not merely regarding her global depressing behavior, but as to her daily activities, especially specific behaviors—that is, how she chose to act hour by hour at home and at work. She made literally hundreds of value judgments that her choices were ineffective in attaining her wants and goals. The initial planning involved her eating at 5:30 P.M., and then performing the following projects, one at a time:

1. Vacuuming the house.
2. Changing the beds.

3. Dusting the guestroom.
4. Straightening up the kitchen.

She reported in a week that there were noticeable improvements in how she felt. She added that she had worked more than the fifteen minutes originally planned and had balanced her checkbook, a project on which she had procrastinated for two months.

In subsequent sessions she reported that she had lost twenty pounds and was now going to Overeaters Anonymous; her co-workers had commented on her weight loss, saying, "You look pretty" and, "You've lost weight." Because she had an intense desire to lose weight, I thought it necessary to help her get a clear perception of herself as thin, rather than exclusively making the plans to lose weight. In other words, she had to lose weight in her *inner* world as well as from her body in the external world. To facilitate this, she formulated affirmations which she would read aloud twice per day:

1. "I weigh 120 pounds."
2. "I look at the positive side of life."
3. "I greet people pleasantly and with a smile."

These affirmations would help her define her wants clearly and help her directly change her thinking behavior (Wubbolding, *Changing Your Life,* 1985). Moreover, she was to spend one minute each day visualizing each of these statements in a specific setting. As time passed, she added more affirmations and changed them:

1. "I am an attractive woman."
2. "I am proud I don't smoke."
3. "I am an intelligent, thinking woman."
4. "I am a healthy, happy 120 pounds."
5. "I drive within the speed limit."

To help her change her Thinking behaviors as well as help her fulfill the needs of power and accomplishment, at her request I prescribed a reading program, as I do for all willing clients whom I counsel. We spent time at nearly every session discussing Stone's *Success through a Positive Mental Attitude,* Maltz's *Psy-*

chocybernetics, and Hill's *Master Key to Riches.* I asked her to mark passages that related to her progress and her efforts to fulfill her needs. Her favorites from *Psychocybernetics* were, "A step in the wrong direction is better than staying on the spot" (page 108) and "Man is like a bicycle. It maintains equilibrium only when going forward" (page 104). A reading program of this kind, called Bibliotherapy, is not unique to Reality Therapy, but can easily be incorporated. One of the earliest works on this topic, from which I have personally benefited, is the classic *Personal Mental Hygiene* by Thomas Verner Moore.

There were, of course, setbacks and times when Jane went to extremes. I explained facetiously that she was an "Extreme-aholic" and that her main task was to maintain balance in her life. When depressed she would sometimes call me at home. I would invariably ask what she is doing and whether moping around the house was helping. This would be followed by my question, "What are you going to do tonight to feel better?" Or sometimes I'd give a simple injunction to "take a brisk walk and call me back in twenty minutes." On the other hand, Jane would occasionally tell me she felt tense and nervous. I would ask her what she was doing and whether it was helping. Then I would either help her make a plan to distract herself or ask her to paradoxically exaggerate the nervousing behavior by tensing up her facial, arm, and leg muscles for five minutes. She learned to do this on her own, and gradually her complaints about tension and nervousness decreased. Sometimes she would go to the other extreme of overexuberance and even was hospitalized. When she felt grandiose she would show it by walking fast, talking loud, driving fast, singing with the car radio on, looking up dozens of words in the dictionary, seeing bizarre symbolism in ordinary comments made by friends, and, in general, thinking that she could conquer any obstacle quickly, especially her dependence on drugs.

My efforts to help Jane contain her exuberance included the formulation of plans centered on the following:

1. Keeping her weight at 128 pounds for a while rather than hurrying to lose more.

2. Walking slowly when she feels excited about something.
3. Talking quietly when she perceives herself talking loudly.
4. Writing small.
5. Looking at the speedometer in the car periodically.
6. Saying, "This is not helping" when she perceives herself driving above the speed limit.
7. Turning down the car radio.
8. Keeping quiet in the car instead of singing.
9. Asking a trusted friend at work to give her feedback about her behavior.
10. Fighting the urge to look up dozens of words in the dictionary.
11. Calling her friend and asking her to go to a singles' group.
12. Eating lunch with co-workers and listening to them rather than talking.
13. Asking her daughter to bring the grandchildren to her house.
14. Taking her grandchildren shopping.
15. Fighting the urge to see symbolism in ordinary comments made by friends and co-workers.
16. Attending to what she is doing at each moment.
17. Reducing "burning desires" simply to "desires."
18. Recording each check in her checkbook promptly and keeping her checkbook balanced.

After approximately forty counseling sessions and many phone calls, Jane still struggles, but is better able to maintain balance in her life. She has a program for moderating her over-exuberancing behaviors as well as a plan for lifting herself out of depressing behaviors. She gets feedback from her friends and co-workers, such as, "You seem at peace with yourself" and "You are working more consistently instead of in spurts." She initiates calls to friends to go to a singles' group. (Once when she was walking her dog, her neighbor recognized the dog but not Jane! Her walk, weight, and smile had changed so dramatically!)

Following Hill's advice in *The Master Key to Riches,* she "goes the extra mile" at work "by taking the initiative" rather than sluggishly avoiding work, as she did formerly. She quit smoking after nearly thirty years of addiction to cigarettes. She has periodically formulated new wants or goals because she constantly achieves them. She has become slim, but is no longer obsessed with weight loss, as she was when she first began. She is even capable of regaining a few pounds without giving in to feelings of upsetness. In short, she has turned her life around and attained a high degree of need fulfillment. Nevertheless Jane struggles, perhaps more than most people, and sometimes has setbacks. But she knows that the struggle is worth it. In her own words, "It's a daily struggle not to be crazy. But I have a program for living."

In a moment of exuberance Jane remarked, "I'm a quintuple winner over drugs, alcohol, cigarettes, overeating, and manic-depression." I asked her if this high level of enthusiasm helped. She commented more realistically, "I'm still working on all of these, especially manic-depression."

One final word should be said about Jane. Unlike many theories of human behavior, in Reality Therapy the manicking and depressing behaviors of Jane are not seen as the cause of other behaviors. In other words, the root of the problem is not the diagnosis of manic-depressive. Manic-Depression, better described as "manicking" and "depressing," are *behaviors.* They are generated to fulfill wants and needs. The work of the Reality Therapist is to help the Janes whom they counsel to identify their wants and needs, *to examine their behaviors, and to formulate better ways to achieve fulfillment and satisfaction.* The manicking and depressing is thus a symptom, not "the root of the problem."

A Married Couple: Helen and Stephen

The second case is included here because it illustrates how Reality Therapy can be used in marriage counseling with a couple who have considerable strength and effective behaviors in their marriage and who are not, therefore, in a state of crisis. When asked if they wanted me to be a marriage or a divorce counselor, they both agreed that they wanted to stay married; they loved each other, but there were issues they could not agree on.

The couple had three children, ages thirty-one, twenty-four, and twelve. The twelve-year-old girl was living at home and doing well in her studies. She was popular at school, had friends, and had several hobbies about which she was "sometimes hot and sometimes cold." The counseling, however, included only the parents—Helen and Stephen.

Helen, fifty-two, had been employed periodically throughout her married life in a managerial position in various travel agencies. At one time she was a partner in a travel agency, but sold her partnership so she could be at home while her daughter, Susan, was young. Recently, she returned to work in another large agency. She saw herself as a professional, capable person sought after by several agencies because of her contacts and her skills in promotion and management. She wanted to continue her career and to maintain the feeling of independence which she felt because of it.

Stephen, fifty-five, was an upper-level manager in a company employing fifteen hundred people. He had worked for the company for eighteen years and had hopes of being promoted to an even higher position. He enjoyed his work and said that he was well respected in the company. Many of his evenings were taken up with social events related to work.

A major area of conflict was in the disparate wants of Helen and Stephen. She wanted her independence as a career woman as well as to be able to rest at home in the evenings alone or with the family. He wanted to attend the business social events with her at his side. He also wanted her to be a more traditional housewife since, as he said, "There is no reason for her to work, as there was when we needed a second income." He conceded that he was close-minded about the possibility of her re-entrance into the world of work. Their behaviors were also quite disparate. Helen did not do the housework as thoroughly as she had formerly, and Stephen was frequently gone in the evenings attending the social meetings related to work. He sometimes had unexpected late meetings, which Helen said "are a source of aggravation for me." As parents, they seemed to relate to their daughter, Susan, in ways that neither felt was effective. Surprisingly, they both agreed that Helen was sometimes too strict, and that Stephen gave in to her too easily. Stephen remarked, "I'm glad Helen's not the union representative at work."

An assessment of their Quality Time revealed that they occasionally went together to Stephen's job-related social functions, school events for Susan, and a periodic meal at an elegant restaurant. There was, however, a time when they were happier and even excited about their life together. When she was a partner in the travel agency he would help with various aspects of the business. They also shared a pleasant life in raising the two older children. They stated that, "We seem to have drifted into a kind of apathy and we'd like to stop this trend as quickly as possible."

Interventions

Application of Level D: Doing alone—Strengthening Activities. In Chapter 8, three of four levels of building relational strength are described in detail. To help Helen and Stephen increase their individual strength within the relationship, I began at the most fundamental level: Doing Alone (Level D). They made many value judgments about their distance from each other and what each, respectively, was doing to increase it. They both took responsibility and determined that many behaviors were ineffective. I helped them make plans to embark on a reading program. She was to read books and magazine articles on men and on the male psyche. He was to read books and magazine articles on the women's movement. I *insisted* that they do this, and that I could help them only if they would carry out this strategy. I made it clear that each of them could benefit from this program if they did this activity separate from the partner. They were able to follow through on this plan to the extent that it was useful in the application of Level C, next.

Application of Level C: Doing Together Alone—Strengthening Activities. It was a few more sessions before Helen and Stephen came to some value judgments about their own Doing Together behaviors. Like many couples, they initiated counseling with the realization that there was something wrong in their relationship. But the realization that it could be changed by changing their behaviors was not immediately evident to them. Nevertheless, they were able to see how the independent nature of their Doing behaviors was driving them apart and further into a condition of ennui about their life together.

So they formulated further plans to take walks three times a week and to discuss their readings. They were to ask each other's opinion and express their own opinion only about their respective readings. During this time there were to be no arguments or discussions that led to controversy.

Further plans included working together on a project around the house for a period of three hours, once a week. This was to be scheduled at a precise time, written down, and discussed in future counseling sessions. Subsequently, Stephen remarked, "The house never looked so good." Helen agreed enthusiastically.

Application of Level B: Communication, Conversation. To enhance communication in a relationship, it is important to help clients define for themselves what they want from each other (Wubbolding, *Reality Therapy Training,* 1985). Very often it is assumed that one partner knows what the other wants. Yet it is quite clear that even after thirty years of marriage, wants are often unclear and uncommunicated. The inner "picture album" is not static or frozen; it is analogous to a movie in which the scenes constantly change. A person's wants today are slightly different from those of yesterday. A person's wants at age fifty-two are different from those at twenty-two. Thus communication about wants requires sustained effort.

To enhance the communication skills of Helen and Stephen, we spent much time on defining, discussing, and evaluating individual wants. Helen wanted respect as a person with ideas and opinions. She wanted Stephen to support her when she disciplined their twelve-year-old daughter. She wanted Stephen to take the initiative in fixing things around the house rather than waiting to be asked. She wanted support in her efforts to be a career person. She also wanted to be consulted before social engagements were made. And, finally, she wanted him to *ask* before he tasted her dessert when they ate in public. Stephen, on the other hand, wanted support rather than sarcasm when they spoke to each other, especially in the presence of their daughter. He stated that he wanted acceptance as a person who tended to be more passive and less assertive than Helen; on his job this was seen as being flexible, so he found it difficult to think of it as a negative quality at home. He wanted her to be enthusiastic about going to social functions connected with his business. And, finally, he wanted at least *some* quiet time in the evenings and on weekends.

They both evaluated their respective wants. Were they realistic and attainable? They decided they could get at least part of what they wanted from each other. Stephen said it would be easy to ask about the dessert, but that it would be more difficult to start projects around the house, at least on a consistent basis. He said he was unaware that he did not support Helen when she disciplined their daughter, but that he recognized the importance of parental unity in this matter. He stated that it is not always possible to consult first with Helen when social engagements arise, but that family gatherings could be handled more satisfactorily. In further evaluation of his wants, Stephen realized that, "Helen has always been blunt," and that it is not realistic to expect or demand that she be supportive of his every wish. One of his most important commitments was to work on accepting her intense desire to have an independent career. It was difficult, he indicated, but he would make the effort.

Helen recognized that unexpected business events were unavoidable and were usually enjoyable. She could settle for better scheduling and consultation around family affairs. She recognized that Stephen has always been known for his flexibility and that, though it got in the way at times, she would never be able to "remake" him. She felt it was quite reasonable that he wanted quiet time and was genuinely willing to provide such opportunities for him. She said that though she felt strongly about wanting his support in her career, she recognized how the attainment of this want would not be soon. She could, however, settle for a sincere effort on Stephen's part.

They began to formulate simple plans at first. Besides keeping

119

their communication on a nonargumentative basis, they agreed to tell each other "I love you" before going to bed. He agreed to talk more directly to her, rather than retreating in a passive way. Helen chose to count to five before saying something when she was angry at him. I had suggested she count to ten, but she said, "I cannot count to ten. I'll count to five." I replied, "Cannot?" She countered with a tone of finality: "Won't!"

In summary, they were able to define and discuss their wants as well as to accept the fact that they must settle for less than total fulfillment. This was followed by formulating short-range plans, which I reinforced.

Application of Level A: Compromise, Avoiding Destructive Arguments. After building the relational strength through *continued* use of Levels C and B, Stephen and Helen were able to compromise. Each felt that he or she was respected in the negotiation and came away with part of what was originally sought. Helen would continue to work, but would not seek or accept the highest level of management possible. She stated, "I really don't want the rat race that much." She added that, after all, she wanted the career only because it gave her more self-esteem and a feeling of contributing. Stephen, on his part, would say yes to only one work-related social event per week which required Helen's presence. He reluctantly agreed to make the compromise of paying someone else to clean the house *and* to pay someone to maintain the outside as well.

The case of Helen and Stephen, summarized above, clearly illustrates the use of Reality Therapy with a couple who has some relational strength present in their marriage. They were able not only to plan, but to follow through on the plans. This required repeated efforts on my part to help them define their wants, make value judgments, and plan Doing behaviors. They were reluctant at first, but eventually chose to change their lives for the better. In this example of short-term counseling, Helen and Stephen learned the process of Reality Therapy and took the initial steps toward change.

In both the case of Jane and that of Helen and Stephen, it should not be concluded that progress was easy or steady. In the growth process experienced in counseling, there are movements forward, plateaus, and setbacks. Reality Therapy requires hard work and effort. Progress is made in Reality Therapy when clients not only understand on an intellectual level, but also come to realize on a deeper level that they are undergoing not "talk-counseling" but "do-counseling." It is at this point that they willingly make plans to change and also follow through with them on a sustained basis.

* 10 *

The Replacement Program: Reality Therapy and Personal Growth

The Replacement Program is an attempt to present a delivery system for personal growth. It defines categories of pictures to be used in the inner world of wants as well as behaviors. A person does not fulfill needs directly, but only through the "picture album" of specific wants. The Replacement Program, therefore, is a categorization of the various possible wants that can be inserted systematically into the world of wants, or "picture album," as well as behaviors. These are specific, precise, and unique for each individual. They consist of "replacements" for the negative, or regressive, elements of failure, weakness, or less control shown by people whose lives are to a greater or lesser extent out of control. Thus Do-it behaviors replace Give-up behaviors, and Positive Symptom behaviors replace Negative Symptom behaviors (see Figure 4). Seeing the right side of the chart with two additional stages helps the practitioner realize that personal growth, mental health, and gaining more effective control over one's life (success, strength, flexibility, and so on) are gradual and developmental. It also opens specific topics for practicing Reality Therapy, especially an exploration of the wants and behaviors of the client.

Furthermore the Replacement Program, made up of Do-it behaviors and Positive Symptom behaviors, comprises specific behaviors that are want and need fulfilling. So it serves many purposes: (1) to help the client identify specific need-fulfilling wants; (2) to help the client identify specific behaviors that would help fulfill needs; and (3) to identify specific behaviors about which to make plans.

Before explaining how Reality Therapy can be seen as a developmental process and as a self-improvement program, it is necessary to understand the categorization of less effective behaviors, as described by Glasser on the classic chart entitled "The Basic Concepts of Reality Therapy." (See Figure 4.) This illustrates how human beings have needs and attempt to fulfill them in successful, strengthening, and flexible ways, thereby gaining control of their lives. When a person performs behaviors that are thus described, they are said to have "effective control" of their lives. On the other hand, some persons attempt to fulfill their needs in ways characterized by failure, weakness, and inflexible behavior, resulting in a lack of effective control of their lives.

The left side of Figure 4 illustrates that losing control, weakness, and so on is a gradual process of deterioration, through Give-up behaviors, Negative Symptom behaviors, and Negative Addiction.

GIVE-UP BEHAVIORS

The first stage of this regression is that of giving up. A person at this point gives up on behaviors described later in this chapter as Do-it behaviors and Positive Symptom behaviors. This stage merges quickly with (Negative) Symptom behaviors, but is characterized by apathy and disinterestedness. It could be either generalized or focused on one element of behavior. For instance, a person could give up on a relationship with one person, resulting in pain, but quickly recover because of other rewarding and satisfying relationships. Such a person retains more effective control than the one whose Give-up decision is generalized to all satisfying relationships.

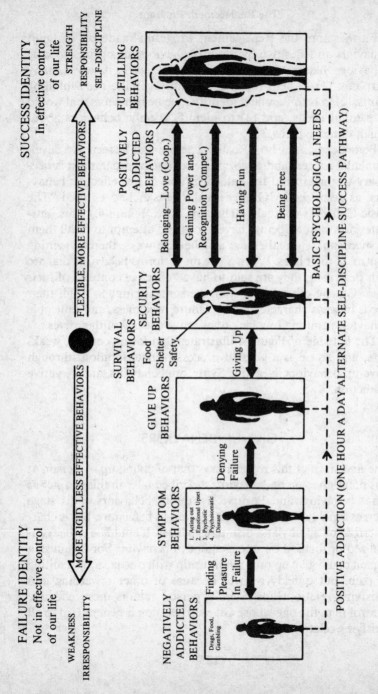

FIGURE 4: THE BASIC CONCEPTS OF REALITY THERAPY

SUCCESS IDENTITY
In effective control
of our life

STRENGTH
RESPONSIBILITY
SELF-DISCIPLINE

FLEXIBLE, MORE EFFECTIVE BEHAVIORS

FAILURE IDENTITY
Not in effective control
of our life

WEAKNESS
IRRESPONSIBILITY

MORE RIGID, LESS EFFECTIVE BEHAVIORS

FULFILLING
BEHAVIORS

POSITIVELY
ADDICTED
BEHAVIORS

Belonging—Love (Coop.)

Gaining Power and
Recognition (Compet.)

Having Fun

Being Free

BASIC PSYCHOLOGICAL NEEDS

SECURITY
BEHAVIORS

Food
Shelter
Safety

SURVIVAL
BEHAVIORS

Giving Up

GIVE UP
BEHAVIORS

Denying Failure

SYMPTOM
BEHAVIORS

1. Acting out
2. Emotional Upset
3. Psychotic
4. Psychosomatic
   Disease

Finding
Pleasure
In Failure

NEGATIVELY
ADDICTED
BEHAVIORS

Drugs, Food,
Gambling

POSITIVE ADDICTION (ONE HOUR A DAY ALTERNATE SELF-DISCIPLINE SUCCESS PATHWAY)

(NEGATIVE) SYMPTOM BEHAVIORS

The second stage of ineffective or less effective control is characterized by one or more negative symptoms:

Acting-Out Behaviors

People acting out choose to violate the rights of others or injure themselves. Mild acting out could be misbehaving in school, breaking the rules of society, and so on. Extreme acting out includes murder, rape, violence, robbery, and the like.

Upsetting Behaviors

The person who depresses, angers, resents, guilts, shames, hates, or generates feelings of anxiety is exhibiting negative, Upsetting behaviors. These Upsetting behaviors are chosen and, as stated in Chapter 1, all behaviors attempt to fulfill wants and satisfy needs. Though some of these choices are effective in controlling others—for example, depressing—they are ineffective in fulfilling needs in a sustained way.

Thinking Behaviors

The most extreme Thinking behavior is psychosing. Some unfortunate people who are unable to meet their needs and wants develop serious mental problems called "psychosis." They become schizophrenic, paranoid, or a host of other types of disturbances. Others choose a milder form of craziness. They obsess, compulse, phobic, or develop other forms of out-of-control behaviors.

Physical Symptoms

Accompanying many failure behaviors are psychosomatic symptoms and illnesses. Many aches and pains have little physiological basis. Every experienced counselor has encountered clients who have been told that their aches are without physical basis. Yet these clients are paining themselves. Their paining, like all the symptoms, are the best behaviors that they can generate at a given time, but they are, nonetheless, ineffective in fulfilling needs. Still other people stress themselves to the point of genuine physiological breakdown. It has long been known that ulcers, heart attacks, high blood pressure, and many "itis's" are a result not so much of what is done to us, but of what we do to ourselves.

It must be noted that the negative symptoms overlap. A person who is angry is also given to acting out at times. Persons compulsing might also depress or headache themselves. Human beings are viewed holistically in Reality Therapy, not simply as people who have isolated problems unrelated to one another. Their out-of-control, failure behaviors—as well as their in-control, successful behaviors—are related one to another.

Negative Addiction

The person addicted to drugs, alcohol, food, gambling, or work lives a life whose focal point is the addiction itself. The addiction is all-absorbing, whether it is indulged frequently or not. If the substance involved is not subject to the power of the person in question, then an addiction is present. There is a saying among alcoholics: "First the man takes the drink. Then the drink takes a drink. Then the drink takes the man."

DO-IT BEHAVIORS

Just as the first phase of ineffective control (weakness, and so forth) is "I give up," resulting in Give-up behaviors, the first phase of taking effective control (strength or success) is reached when a person desires to "do it." (See Figure 5.) When someone wishes to change, to improve and, even more, when plans are implemented, this stage of control has been reached. The desire might be very minimal, but it is a major step and often follows

Needs

Belonging

Power, Self-worth, etc.

Fun

Freedom

Survival

Do-It Behaviors

"I want to improve."

"I want to change my life."

"I want to have a better relationship."

Positive Symptom Behaviors

1. Constructive Actions

   a. assertive

   b. altruistic

2. Positive Feelings

   a. trust

   b. self-confidence

   c. patience

   d. adequacy

   e. etc.

3. Rational and Positive Thinking

4. Healthful Activities

   a. diet

   b. exercise

   c. hygiene

   d. etc.

FIGURE 5: REPLACEMENT PROGRAM

the extensive and skillful use of at least the first several procedures of Reality Therapy.

Following are worksheets with sample questions you can use to elicit a desire to change. They are practice sheets for developing further questions that can be used in the discussion of the first stage of strength as it relates to the practice of Reality Therapy (exploration of wants and behaviors). Try to develop other questions, too. The questions are illustrations and are not intended to be used blindly in every counseling situation. The worksheets are exercises in question formulation, not in the art of counseling. After all, the "art of counseling" includes not only knowing how to ask questions, but how to ask *well-timed* questions, as well as many other skills.

Questions Appropriate for the Practice of Reality Therapy ("What do you want and really want?")

1. Do you want to change?
2. Do you want to change your life?
3. Do you want to change how you feel, what you do, your attitudes (how you think about things)?
4. If you changed, how would your life be better?
5. If you changed, would you feel better?
6. What would you have in your life if you changed?
7. What do you want in your life that you're not getting?

8. _____

9. _____

10. _____

11. _____

12. _____

13. _____

14. _____

15. _____

16. _____
17. _____
18. _____
19. _____
20. _____

Questions Appropriate for the Practice of Reality Therapy
("What are you doing?")

1. Describe the last time you got along with _____.
2. Describe the last time you had a good laugh.
3. Describe a time in your life when you felt enthusiastic about living. What were you doing?
4. Describe the last time you felt a sense of achievement. What were you doing?
5. Describe the last time you had a sense of freedom. What were you doing?
6. Describe what you did in the last week during which you had a sense of "being in charge."
7. Describe what you are doing on an ongoing basis in any relationship which you would say is "relatively free of conflict."

8. _____
9. _____
10. _____
11. _____
12. _____
13. _____
14. _____
15. _____

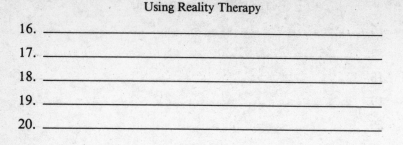

16. _____

17. _____

18. _____

19. _____

20. _____

POSITIVE SYMPTOM BEHAVIORS

Positive Symptom behaviors is parallel to Negative Symptom behaviors. Failure and weakness are recognized through the less effective efforts to fulfill needs by acting out, "upsetting," psychosing, or sicking; so, also, control of one's life (strength and success) are recognizable and enhanced by opposite symptoms.

Constructive Actions

Just as a person whose life is uncontrolled fulfills his or her needs ineffectively through acting-out behaviors, the strong person fulfills needs without damaging him- or herself or others. Constructive actions consist of two kinds: assertive and contributing. Assertive behaviors are designed to help in self-expression, contribute to self-enhancement, and so on. Alberti and Emmons (1974) define assertive behavior as that which "enables a person to act in his own best interest, to stand up for himself without undue anxiety, to express his honest feelings comfortably, or to exercise his own rights without denying the right of others. . . ." In short, it could be said that assertive behaviors "get you what you want without hurting others."

Contributing behaviors, on the other hand, though not contradictory to assertive behaviors, are more explicitly designed to contribute to the welfare of others—for example, joining a volunteer organization or doing favors for people. Many actions are a mixture of both assertive and contributing behaviors. When people are employed in jobs they enjoy, they feel that they are *getting what they want for themselves* and at the same time are *contributing* to the welfare of society.

Following are questions about constructive actions that relate to the exploration of behavior and to the evaluation procedures. Again, add further questions, as suitable.

Questions Appropriate for the Exploration of Current Behaviors ("What are you doing?")

1. Describe the last time you stood up for yourself.
2. Describe the last time you approached someone, knowing you might be rejected.
3. Describe the last time you acted without feeling that you needed someone else's permission.
4. Describe the last time you had fun alone . . . with someone else. What did you do?
5. How many jobs have you looked for this week?
6. Have you ever worked for a volunteer organization? Describe what you did.
7. Do you do any favors for your brothers and sisters? What kind? When?

8. _____
9. _____
10. _____
11. _____
12. _____
13. _____
14. _____
15. _____
16. _____
17. _____
18. _____

19. _____

20. _____

Questions Appropriate for Evaluation
("Is what you're doing helping you?")

1. Did it help you when you asserted yourself in that situation? How?
2. Was there a sense of satisfaction in reaching out to someone? Was it at least "different" for you?
3. Did you enjoy having fun? Describe it.
4. Would it help you to have friends? How?
5. Would it help you to be around more people? In what way?
6. How would it help to have a job?
7. What is in your best interest to do in this matter? In the interest of your family?

8. _____

9. _____

10. _____

11. _____

12. _____

13. _____

14. _____

15. _____

16. _____

17. _____

18. _____

19. _____

20. _____

Positive Feelings

Just as out-of-control persons fulfill their needs in an ineffective manner by depressing, shaming, guilting, resenting, angering, worrying, and so on, people with a sense of control seek to fulfill their needs in strong or successful ways by joying, self-confidencing, self-accepting, patiencing, adequacing, and the like. Following are sample questions relating to positive feelings, based on the exploration of behavior and evaluation procedures.

Questions and Injunctions Appropriate for the Exploration of Behavior (What are you doing?")

1. Describe the last time you felt good. What were you doing?
2. Describe the last time you had a sense of satisfaction from your job. What were you doing on the job?
3. Describe the last time you felt self-confident. What were you doing?
4. How were you acting when you and your spouse were happily married?
5. What did you do today to feel better? Describe it in detail.
6. Describe how other people act who are happy or who seem to enjoy life.
7. Have you read any books about happy people?

8. _____
9. _____
10. _____
11. _____
12. _____
13. _____
14. _____
15. _____

16. _____

17. _____

18. _____

19. _____

20. _____

Questions Appropriate for Evaluation
("Is what you're doing helping you?")

1. Does it help or hurt to nurse the negative feelings? To tell your friend about them? How?
2. What effect does it have to tell everyone how lousy you feel?
3. What would it take for you to have a sense of satisfaction on the job?
4. When you show your resentment by refusing to talk, does that bring you closer to your spouse?
5. Does telling people, "I can't," add or subtract from your self-confidence?
6. What effect will reading positive books have on your feelings?
7. If you fail in your efforts what's the worst thing that could happen?

8. _____

9. _____

10. _____

11. _____

12. _____

13. _____

14. _____

15. _____

16. _____

17. _____

18. _____

19. _____

20. _____

Rational and Positive Thinking

Weak and ineffective people often seek to fulfill their needs by withdrawing from the world and by "living in a world of their own." Such people "psychose" themselves. Others engage in a lesser form of disturbance: negativistic thinking (the eternal pessimist—that is, the man who wears both a belt and suspenders!). The converse of this negative symptom is the positive symptom characterized by rational thinking. Rational thinkers can think problems through and face unpleasant situations without feeling overwhelmed. They are open to experience and learn from it, can look on the bright side, display a sense of humor, have what Stone (1977) calls a "positive mental attitude," and can evaluate the world in a responsible manner.

Following are sample questions relating to rational and positive thinking, based on exploration of current behaviors and evaluation procedures.

Questions and Injunctions Appropriate for the Exploration of Behaviors ("What are you doing?")

1. Describe the last time you observed him or her doing something positive.
2. What kind of people and situations do you enjoy? Describe a recent time when you were in such a situation.
3. Describe a time that you faced up to a difficult situation when you felt like running away from it.
4. Do you read any positive-thinking books?

135

5. What advantages do you have going for you which you could exploit in the near future?
6. What do you do differently now from what you did five years ago?
7. Have you changed your thinking about a topic in the last two years? Which topic?

8. _____
9. _____
10. _____
11. _____
12. _____
13. _____
14. _____
15. _____
16. _____
17. _____
18. _____
19. _____
20. _____

Questions Appropriate for Evaluation
("Is what you're doing helping you?")

1. How does it help to see the positive side of things? Of this person, and so on?
2. What does your child, spouse, boss, employee, and so on do that you approve of? Describe a specific instance.
3. How do happy people view similar situations?
4. Will it really help you to make such dire predictions about that situation? How does it help or hurt?
5. What are the worst and best things that will happen if you change?

6. Will breaking the "dumb rule" really get you what you want?
7. How is griping helping?

8. _____
9. _____
10. _____
11. _____
12. _____
13. _____
14. _____
15. _____
16. _____
17. _____
18. _____
19. _____
20. _____

Healthful Activities

Many people attempt to resolve frustrations by sicking themselves through psychosomatic illnesses or symptoms. Others fail to take care of their physical needs by refusing to eat properly or failing to exercise or even take care of their hygienic needs. Any experienced counselor has encountered clients who are enmeshed in several of these subsymptoms. In my own counseling I ask such people—*rather, I prescribe*—that they take care of their basic hygienic needs. I insist that they at least make a plan to bathe on the day they come to see me; this is for my benefit as well as theirs.

The positive symptom is again the converse of the negative psychosomatic symptoms. The person who has effective control (strong, successful) eats properly, exercises regularly, and so on.

Of course, the word "proper" should be understood in a very wide sense. Yet if clients give sufficient time and energy even to these basic forms of physical activity, they often show dramatic improvements.

Following are sample questions relating to healthful activities, based on the exploration of behavior and evaluation procedures.

Questions and Injunctions Appropriate for the Exploration of Behavior ("What are you doing?")

1. Describe the last time you took a walk, stretched your muscles, got exercise.
2. Did you take care of your hygiene today?
3. What did you eat yesterday?
4. What kind of friendships did you form when you had that hobby? Describe one in detail.
5. When did you have a sense of satisfaction or achievement about the way you looked? Describe your appearance at that time.
6. When you dress up, what kind of clothes do you wear? Give a precise description.
7. What did you weigh when you felt good about yourself? Describe what you did to maintain that weight.

8. _____
9. _____
10. _____
11. _____
12. _____
13. _____
14. _____
15. _____
16. _____

17. _____
18. _____
19. _____
20. _____

Questions Appropriate for Evaluation
("Is what you're doing helping you?")

1. Will it really help you *not* to walk, *not* to stretch your muscles, *not* to get exercise?
2. Will lounging around all day in your bathrobe get you what you want?
3. How could you benefit from exercise? Describe the benefits in detail.
4. Does "cleaning up" help or hurt other people? How? Would it help you?
5. How would your life be different if you were thinner?
6. What is being overweight stopping you from doing?
7. How would more variety and fun help you?

8. _____
9. _____
10. _____
11. _____
12. _____
13. _____
14. _____
15. _____
16. _____
17. _____
18. _____

19. _____

20. _____

CASE EXAMPLE: JANE

Chapter 9 describes Jane. Here is her progress in the context of a Do-it person with Positive Symptoms behaviors:

Jane stated that she wanted to improve, to change her life, and get the feeling of being in charge of how she was living rather than being at the mercy of drugs, food, depressions, and the like. This global commitment to "I'll do it" led her to more specific wants related to each positive symptom.

She stated that among her explicit wants were desires to assert herself by having a secure job, financial security, acceptance by other people, and better control of her personal life (for example, neatness of her home, control of her checkbook and spending). She wanted to make contributions to others through productive work like helping her grandchildren and painting. She also wanted to feel positive about herself—that is, that she was a competent person. Jane described how she wanted more than anything else to be sane and "even tempered," neither too high nor too low in her moods. And, finally, she wanted to maintain her weight at a healthful level, which would make her more attractive.

The importance of defining wants related to needs is thus obvious. The attainment of wants and the ensuing effective need fulfillment is known by the client and the therapist (as well as by the employer, friends, and relatives of the client) when the positive symptoms become observable. Consequently, when Jane began to perform more satisfactorily on the job, save money, balance her checkbook, and so forth, she could then be called a person with Positive Symptom behaviors. She moved beyond the wanting state—that is, the "I'll do it" position—to the point at which she could execute behaviors to get what she wanted.

In moving to Positive Symptom behaviors, Jane was able to exhibit more Feeling behaviors such as self-confidence, trust, and humility. The latter was, for her, a positive symptom that served to balance a tendency toward grandiosity. At times she tended to believe she could accomplish anything she set out to do. Humility and fear were thus positive feelings for her. She likewise showed the positive symptom of rationality by making plans and *following through on them* to drive slowly, evaluate decisions, and consult with a friend periodically. The execution of these plans helped her maintain the symptom of rational thinking. Lastly, Jane succeeded in her exercise and weight program. This has always been for her and many others a barometer for other symptoms and for effective need fulfillment. It is something that is a struggle involving measurable advances and retreats, successes and failures.

In summary, it is helpful to see the healthy personality as developmental and the weak personality as gradually regressive. Others (Erickson 1968, Sheehy 1974) have described normal growth and development in terms of stages through which human beings must pass. The model of development discussed in this chapter describes symptoms of a strong, healthy person at any stage of development. Whether a person is very young and healthy or very old and infirm there are needs which must be fulfilled. These needs are fulfilled when the positive symptoms are present: constructive action, positive feelings, rational thinking, and healthful activities.

* 11 *

Applications to the World of Work

The process of Reality Therapy can also be used in the workplace by managers or supervisors. Applying it to the supervisor-supervisee relationship, Glasser and Karrass (1980) describe Reality Performance Management (RPM), or Reality Management (Wubbolding 1984), as "a way of working with employees that quickly gets them to direct their attention to their behavior, to what they do and think, much more than what they feel. By using the techniques of RPM, the manager learns to push employees gently towards RPM's key concept: *I am responsible for what I do.*"

They also describe the components as follows:

1. Establishing and keeping a good relationship with each subordinate.
2. Using that ongoing relationship to get the employee to lay on the table what he or she is or isn't doing right.
3. Asking the employee to evaluate his or her behavior in terms of its effect on the job to be done and on fellow workers.
4. Negotiating with the employee to develop a realistic, workable plan to handle the situation in a better way.

5. Getting the employee to agree to follow the plan and providing an equal commitment to help if your help is needed.
6. Asking for and accepting no excuses for why a job cannot be done better.
7. Criticizing in a constructive, nonpunitive, fashion.
8. Not giving up easily. (The good manager is a model for the dogged belief that there is always a better way—and shows it by not giving up.)

In my teaching of effective management skills, I have enlarged these eight components to include several of the ideas contained in Chapters 2 through 6, some of which include applications of Reality Therapy as a counseling method. Here is how these ideas have been incorporated.

A Good Relationship

Establishing and maintaining a good relationship with each subordinate can be done by:

1. Asking About the "Wants" of the Supervisee. The manager helps the employees set goals for themselves—career goals or project goals. These can be on a daily, weekly, monthly, yearly, or lifetime basis. Explored also is what the employees want that they are getting or not getting for themselves, from the job, or from their co-workers. There is a wealth of "counseling," coaching, or supervising material that can be uncovered by a manager or supervisor who can skillfully ask questions about wants (goals).

2. Determining the "Needs" of Supervisees. Relating wants to human needs is helpful. This need not be overdone, but simple questions such as, "Would completing the project give you a sense of satisfaction and accomplishment?" or "Would being on time help you feel more accepted by the rest of the staff?" are helpful.

143

3. Telling Employees Exactly What is Expected of Them. A written job description is necessary, but it is rarely sufficient for employees to know where they stand on a daily or weekly basis. Performance reviews are also necessary, but the content should not be a surprise to the employee when a formal review conference is held. Blanchard and Johnson (1982) speak of "one-minute praising" and "one-minute reprimands." These are useful, but often more detailed conferences are needed to describe what is expected, to give praise, or to point toward a better way to do a job.

4. Clarifying Employees' Perceptions. The effective manager asks how the employees see themselves in the workplace—as hardworking, committed, efficient, prompt, attentive to detail, self-initiating, and so on, or the opposite. How employees see the job and the company (or agency) can be explored by asking questions such as, "What part in the company do you see yourself playing?"

5. Practicing the ABCs. No matter how upset a subordinate is at a given moment, the manager should always be *C*ourteous and *C*alm. (This is, of course, an ideal, for no one implements all his or her ideas perfectly.) *D*etermination, *E*nthusiasm, and *F*irmness extend and complete the ABCs. Glasser and Karrass (1980) state that a manager needs a "dogged determination" that there is a better way to do things. There should also be an enthusiasm for the company, for the goals, for the work performed by the employees, as well as a firmness in applying rules and consequences.

6. Doing the Unexpected. Praising them at unexpected moments, discussing successes rather than failures, looking to the next project, or making another plan when employees expect a reprimand can be very effective tools for forming supportive relationships with employees.

7. Sharing Yourself. Managers can describe their own ideas that have worked in the past. Though this is a tactic easily overused, it can be helpful if well timed. Such suggestions are most

144

effective if employees do not feel put down or patronized. If the earlier parts of this step are used first, employees will be more open to suggestions.

8. Make the Interview Fun, if Possible.   A manager is, in many ways, a counselor helping people direct their lives, feel better about themselves, and perform more effectively on the job. These efforts are aided by a sense of humor. If laughter is "the best medicine," it is also, a very effective management tool.

Laying It on the Table

A manager can use that ongoing relationship to get employees to lay on the table what they are or are not doing right. In this component, the manager asks the employees to use their mind as a television camera to tell exactly what happened. The key is to aid them in being specific and precise, rather than vague. All hint of criticism and judgment is omitted at this stage. The manager should avoid asking, "Why did you fail?" in any form. Such "Why?" questions result in defensiveness and self-justification.

Self-Evaluation

The manager should ask employees to evaluate their own behavior. This component is the most powerful of all, for the manager *asks* the employee to examine what they are doing that is helping or hurting. Instead of *telling,* the manager first asks for an evaluation—not of the behavior of other people, but of the behavior of the employees themselves. "Is coming late to work really helping?" It is perfectly acceptable for a manager to tell employees what seems to be helping and hurting. But lecturing *endlessly* is largely ineffective unless there is an internal evaluation by the employee.

More specifically, the criteria for evaluation are: (1) the job to be done, (2) the effect on other people, (3) the helpfulness in getting what they want; and (4) the rules of the company or agency. For example, these questions could be asked concerning tardiness: "Is it helping to get the project done on time when you

145

take an hour and a half for lunch?" "What effect does it have on other people when you come forty-five minutes late for work? Do you think they feel better or worse toward you?" "You want a promotion. Will being late help you advance in the company?" "What's the rule about starting time? Is it against the rules to be late?" Not every one of the criteria is appropriate in every situation, but a skillful manager or supervisor can develop ingenious ways to help employees examine what they are doing and distinguish between helpful and harmful behaviors.

Negotiations

The manager negotiates with employees to develop a realistic, workable plan to handle the situation in a better way. There are many characteristics of a plan, as described in Chapter 3. Glasser and Karrass (1980) appropriately stress that it be "realistic and workable." The plan should be attainable for the employee. The employee who is habitually tardy will hardly be prompt "from now on. . . ." "From now on" is a very long time. Such an ineffective worker can often make a plan for one week only, or even for a few days. (This minimal change should be reinforced and extended with added supervision.) After making the value judgment that tardiness is not helping, the manager might ask, "Would you be willing to make a plan to be here at 8:00 A.M. every day for a week? Can you handle such a plan for five days?" The plan is thus simple, attainable, workable, dependent only on the employee, firm, and so on.

Follow-Through

The manager gets employees to follow the plan and provides an equal commitment to help, if help is needed. The firmness of the plan is illustrated by this component. The plan could be written down and/or a follow-up meeting scheduled. Consequences could be determined or simply described by the manager. Sometimes it is sufficient to reiterate the plan verbally. This and the other steps are useful in conducting performance reviews; I recommend that they be conducted every ninety days. Even these quarterly reviews are hardly enough if managers have a grasp of the principles described in the chapter. They will have a wealth of material to discuss with each employee.

No Excuses

The manager asks for and accepts no excuses for why a job cannot be done better. There are instances when the first five components are followed perfectly, and still the employee does not follow the plan. Most often, however, one of the earlier components was not clearly or sufficiently used. Employees don't follow through on plans for several reasons: (1) they didn't want to do the plan (the first component was lacking); (2) they haven't decided that the "irresponsible" behavior is irresponsible—that is, not helping (the third component was lacking); or (3) the plan was not a good plan (the fourth component was lacking). In any case, it is helpful to return to earlier components and aim for a better, workable plan. Above all, the caveat here is to ask for and accept no excuses. If employees are asked why they failed, they will welcome the opportunity to explain why in endless detail. This "why" will often be an explanation (excuses) of how uncontrollable forces or other people were the causes of the failure. How many of us—employees, supervisors, managers, or presidents of companies—like to admit, "I failed because I did not plan adequately"? Rather it is easier to blame co-workers, subordinates, the competition, the government—the list is endless. The best way to avoid excuses is to avoid asking, "Why did you fail?"

Consequences

Don't criticize or argue, but allow or impose consequences. It is useless to argue about the reasonableness of rules or about "fairness" or "unfairness." The rule of thumb is, "Don't argue." Rather, look to the future. And if consequences are to be imposed, they should be done so without apology or offering lengthy and undue justification. Under no circumstances should employees be demeaned, belittled, or humiliated. This will result in even more negative behaviors.

Persistence

The manager doesn't give up easily. As in counseling, he or she keeps the picture in mind of being capable of helping employees perform better. To remove this picture is to give up. Also, there are difficult moments for any manager, and there is a temptation for some to give up on these principles when they don't work perfectly and immediately. Reality Management, however, requires practice, effort, and the development of good questioning skills. This is brought about through study, training, and practice.

Case Example: Louis

The following dialogue is hypothetical and represents several supervisory sessions condensed into one. Louis, two years away from retirement, is perceived by his manager to be "semiretired" on the job. He does the bare minimum, talks constantly about retirement, and criticizes the company in front of younger employees. He has been with the company twenty-eight years. The session begins:

MGR: Hello, Lou, how are you today?

LOUIS: Tired. Stayed up to watch the movie.

MGR: That's exactly what I want to talk to you about.

LOUIS: The movie? Did you watch it?

MGR: No, I wanted to ask you about the amount of energy you've been giving to the job.

LOUIS: I do my job! I've worked here twice as long as you have!

MGR: That's right! I've learned a lot from you. And I wanted to talk to you about how you're doing *now*.

LOUIS: Well, as I said, I do my job.

MGR: And you're looking forward to retirement?

LOUIS: You bet! I've got two more years.

MGR: Lou, how would you compare your work habits in the last few weeks with how they were ten or fifteen years ago when you were on your way up in the company?

148

LOUIS: You mean like that report you returned to me because of the mistakes I made?

MGR: That's a good example. How did that compare with how you did reports years ago?

LOUIS: It was sloppier.

MGR: What happens when reports are sloppy?

LOUIS: Well, they have to be redone.

MGR: What effect does it have on the younger workers when you turn in sloppy reports and come late for work?

LOUIS: They don't say anything.

MGR: But what effect does it have?

LOUIS: They probably think, "If he can get away with it why can't I?"

MGR: Exactly! Deep down inside, do you think you're working as hard as you can?

LOUIS: Not really. But I've given twenty-eight years to the company.

MGR: Lou, I know that. And I'm not trying to minimize it. In fact, I'd like to ask you, what kind of worker do you want to be for the last two years? What do you want people to say when you retire?

LOUIS: I want them to think of me as a good worker.

MGR: The young workers will remember the last two years more than the first twenty-eight.

LOUIS: You're right.

MGR: And, Lou, what do you want to be able to say about yourself? "I coasted into retirement, loafing the last two years and wasn't much of an example for the younger workers?"

LOUIS: Hell no! That sounds awful! Is that what you think of me?

MGR: I'm definitely afraid it could happen. What do you want to be able to say when you retire?

LOUIS: "I worked hard up to the end and was an example to the younger workers."

MGR: Oh! So you feel strongly about how you could serve as an example to the younger workers. Would you like to be proud of yourself and have others be proud they worked with you?

LOUIS: Yes, I definitely would.

MGR: Is loafing and complaining going to help you attain that goal?

LOUIS: No! Not really.

MGR: Lou, I'd like these things for you, too. I see you as a potential influence for good or ill in this office. It's your choice as to how you'll work and what you'll be for the next two years.

LOUIS: I guess you're right.

MGR: Lou, could you reverse your present trend . . . really give it hell for one week?

LOUIS: Sure. I can do that.

MGR: How, specifically, would you do that?

LOUIS: I'll be on time and stop complaining from now on.

MGR: How about just for one week?

LOUIS: Sure, I can handle that.

MGR: Lou, would you be on time and speak positively about the company a couple of times a day? Maybe tell someone why you chose to work here rather than go elsewhere when you had the opportunity.

LOUIS: That's a good idea.

MGR: Let's talk again in a week to see how it's going. Okay?

LOUIS: Okay. Thanks.

This dialogue is not intended to prove that using these skills always produces a perfect result or automatically helps every employee make a 180-degree turnaround. Yet it is not totally fabricated. It illustrates many of the role-play sessions I have had in training sessions for effective management skills, and which managers report take place when they use these steps. But, more specifically, the dialogue is intended to provide a brief illustration of how the various ideas can be used "to push employees gently toward the key concept: I am responsible for what I do."

The following pages have two activities in which you are asked to apply these steps. The first is the Job Examination Personal Profile (JEPP). The questions will help you apply the ideas to the job. You are asked to fill in the answers in order to get a "feel" for this method, as well as help you increase your own job effectiveness. The more specific you are, the more helpful will be the exercise.

The second activity involves cases which serve as practice sessions to help you formulate questions for several of the components used in the practice of Reality Management.

Job Examination Personal Profile (JEPP)

These questions are designed to help you:

1. Determine your relationship to the job.
2. Examine your effectiveness on the job.
3. Explore and select possible ways to better fulfill needs and wants on the job.

Answer the questions as honestly and completely as you can. Do not be concerned about "right" or "wrong" answers. The correct answers are what you think and feel.

NEEDS

1. Which of your four needs (belonging, power, fun, freedom) was met on a continuing basis in the last week? How?
2. To what extent are you satisfied with the way this need was fulfilled? What exactly were you satisfied with? Dissatisfied with?
3. What needs do you want to fulfill more effectively on the job?
4. Which needs can you *realistically* meet more effectively on the job? How?
5. In answering the "How?" questions above, do you have control over the elements that need to be changed?
6. Did you have a sense of belonging on the job this

past week? Did you feel part of the company or agency? What was the occasion?

7. Did you have a feeling of achievement or accomplishment on the job this past week? What was the occasion?

8. Did you have a laugh on the job in the past week? What was the occasion?

9. Did you have the opportunity to act independently, on your own, or to make a job-related decision in the last week? What was the occasion?

10. To what degree are you willing to put forth an effort to more effectively fulfill your needs for belonging, power or achievement, fun, and freedom on the job?

WANTS

1. List what you are getting from your job that is satisfying to you.

2. Is there anyone on the job you call a friend? Who?

3. Is there anyone you would like to be closer to on the job? List him or her.

4. Is there a task that you are working on at the present time from which you derive a feeling of accomplishment? Describe it.

5. Do you want to get a greater feeling of accomplishment from the task? Describe how this could be brought about?

6. Is there a person with whom you can express humor on the job? Who is it? What helps both of you to have fun?

7. Do you want to have more fun and laughs on the job? How?

8. Do you want to act more independently on the job? How?

9. Do you want to make more decisions that "stick"? Which ones?

10. Do you want more or less supervision on the job? What do you want from your supervisor/manager that you are getting? Not getting? Be specific.

11. What is there in yourself that you would like to change in the next week?

12. What would help you to be a more effective employee?

13. To what extent are you willing to make the effort?

14. What work-related goals could you set for the next week? Month?

15. Are you willing to tell others what you want that would help you fulfill your four needs? Whom would you tell?

PERCEPTIONS—HOW YOU LOOK AT THINGS

1. What do you like about the way you do your job?

2. What do you dislike about the way you do your job?

3. Describe the positive elements about your company or agency.

4. To what extent can you tolerate the negative elements?

5. How do you see yourself as a worker? Efficient, inefficient, self-initiating, waiting to be told, dependable, not dependable, prompt, tardy, ambitious, laid-back, creative, uncreative? Be specific; relate your view of yourself to the last week.

6. How do you see your relationship to your co-workers? Cooperative, uncooperative, helpful, hurtful, friendly, aloof, kind, sarcastic? Relate your view to the last week.

7. How do you see your relationship to your manager/supervisor? Cooperative, uncooperative,

helpful, comfortable, uncomfortable, close, distant? Relate your view to the last week.

8. How do you see yourself fitting into the company or agency?
9. How do you think your manager/supervisor sees you?
10. How do you think your family members see you and your position in the company/agency?

DOING BEHAVIORS AND EVALUATION

1. Describe one work activity performed in the last week wherein you gained a sense of belonging, power or accomplishment, fun, or freedom. Be specific.
2. Describe what you did in that activity that helped you, your co-workers, or the organization. Be specific.
3. Describe one work activity performed in the last week that did not go well for you. Be specific.
4. What did you do that had a negative effect on what you want, on your co-workers, or on the job to be done. Be specific.
5. List in two columns the activities for the week which you evaluate as plus and minus based on *your own* performance. Check the ones you will work on improving in the next week.

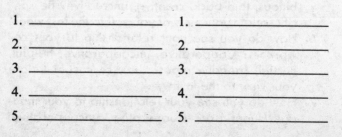

PLUS	MINUS
1. _____	1. _____
2. _____	2. _____
3. _____	3. _____
4. _____	4. _____
5. _____	5. _____

PLANNING AND COMMITMENT

1. What firm plan will you make *now* to fulfill one need more effectively and to get what you want on the job? Duration of plan: one week.
2. What firm plan will you make *now* to help co-workers feel a sense of belonging or achievement on the job? Duration of plan: one week.
3. What firm plan will you make *now* to do your job more efficiently? Duration of plan: one week.
4. What firm plan will you make *now* to show initiative? Duration of plan: one week.
5. What firm plan will you make *now* to make the workplace more pleasant? Duration of plan: one week.

NO EXCUSES, NO CRITICISM, REASONABLE CONSEQUENCES

1. How could you sabotage each of your plans? Be specific.
2. Are you genuinely and truly committed to your plans? Use a complete sentence to answer this question, not one word.
3. What excuses *could* you (but would not) make for not following through on your plans?
4. Are you willing to scratch out your excuses above?
5. Describe your day on the job if you did not criticize yourself or others.

HANGING IN THERE, NOT GIVING UP EASILY

1. Describe what "dogged belief that there is a better way" means to you. Apply this phrase to a specific work situation.

2. In the last week, did you give up on getting what you want, being involved with co-workers, or getting a job done? How? Be specific.
3. To what extent are you willing to change your behavior—that is, to follow through on your plans for the next week?
4. How could you energize yourself for work before you arrive in the morning? Are you willing to change your morning habits? In what way?
5. When and how often are you willing to examine your own wants, Doing behaviors, and plans so as to more satisfactorily fulfill your needs and wants and contribute to your co-workers and the organization?

The JEPP is intended to help you examine your own needs, wants, perceptions, and behaviors as they apply to the workplace. As in counseling, managers and supervisors can more effectively apply these concepts and procedures to subordinates if they have first applied them to themselves. Also, the questions can be used in or adapted to supervisory or "counseling" sessions.

Case Examples

Following are three cases, presented here to help you apply the concepts and components of Reality Management to specific instances. Formulate the questions, plans, and so on for each case. Remember, however, that such questions should not be used indiscriminately in the "real world." These cases represent a practice activity, not the fine art of managing and supervising people in real-life situations.

CASE 1: JODY

This case is similar to Louis, described earlier; refer back to those pages for questions which could also be useful here, and formulate your own questions also.

Jody is going to retire in two years, and does the bare minimum, avoids responsibility, refuses to take initiative. Jody's reports are incomplete and late. When speaking at meetings, Jody usually gives excuses about why something can't be done. Some of the younger employees around Jody are complaining about Jody's negative attitude, while others are starting to imitate Jody.

Relationships (wants, needs, perceptions), 3 questions:

1. _____
2. _____
3. _____

Current Behavior, 3 questions:

1. _____
2. _____
3. _____

Evaluation, 3 questions:

1. _____
2. _____
3. _____

Planning: Make a plan of action. Does it fulfill the characteristics of a good plan?

Excuses: How would you deal with excuses?

157

CASE 2: CHRIS

Chris, a sales manager for your company, has four salespeople reporting. Sales are down $200,000 for the year. Chris blames the economy and says the salespeople are doing the best they can. Yet Chris rarely has sales meetings; has no added incentives for them; discusses on the telephone important items that should be discussed in person with the sales representatives; and takes time off work to play golf, go shopping, and take care of personal affairs.

Relationships (wants, needs, perceptions), 3 questions:

1. _____

2. _____

3. _____

Current Behavior, 3 questions:

1. _____

2. _____

3. _____

Evaluation, 3 questions:

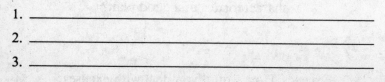

1. _____

2. _____

3. _____

Planning: Make a plan of action. Does it fulfill the characteristics of a good plan?

Excuses: How would you deal with excuses?

CASE 3: LEE

Lee works at the counter for a retail company, dealing with the public and also has some desk responsibilities. Lee complains that the other employees don't carry their load. Lee says s/he does more than her/his share. Yet others say Lee loafs at times, and that Lee complains to the other employees and even complains openly in front of the public who seek service at the counter.

Relationships (wants, needs, perceptions), 3 questions:

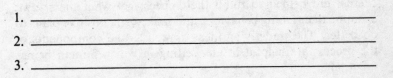

1. _____
2. _____
3. _____

Current Behavior, 3 questions:

1. _____
2. _____
3. _____

Evaluation, 3 questions:

1. _____
2. _____
3. _____

Planning: Make a plan of action. Does it fulfill the characteristics of a good plan?

Excuses: How would you deal with excuses?

In summary, it is clear that Reality Management is the application of Reality Therapy's Cycle of Counseling to the managing and supervising of workers. Managers and supervisors deal with persons facing problems similar to those encountered by professional counselors. At work, or in counseling, employees (or clients) are helped to fulfill their needs; get what they want; examine their Doing behaviors; and make firm, positive plans to do better. The underlying ideas as well as the components of the process are helpful in any setting in which human beings function.

* 12 *

Questioning and Questions

This chapter consists of two separate components: (1) a discussion of questioning skills—how questions are used by a therapist in the practice of Reality Therapy; and (2) special questions that are frequently asked about the theory and practice of Reality Therapy.

In using Reality Therapy, it is important to develop extensive questioning skills. The emphasis on questioning sets Reality Therapy apart from most other methods which utilize reflective techniques. Instead of responding, "You are angry," a Reality Therapist would say, "What did you *do* the last time you were angry?" Instead of telling someone that a behavior is harmful, the Reality Therapist is more inclined to ask if the behavior is helpful or hurtful. I use the phrase "more inclined" because it should not be concluded that statements and reflective techniques are *never* used. Reality Therapy should not be viewed as a rigid system wherein there is only one appropriate skill. However, more questions are generally asked in Reality Therapy than in other counseling and communication methods.

The Purposes of Questioning

Questions are not asked aimlessly. The therapist has several clear and distinct goals.

161

1. To Enter the Inner World of Clients

In asking clients what they want, what they really want, what they are doing, what are their plans, and so on, the therapist attempts to see the world as their clients see it. Thus a high level of empathy (friendship) is shown less by reflective listening than by skillful questioning. And so it is important to develop many ways to ask questions. For instance, I have found it useful to ask clients what they *really* want by asking what they would have if they got what they wanted. When parents say they want their child to come in early, study in school, talk in a friendly way to other members of the family, do the assigned chores, and so on, I ask them what they would have if their child did all of those things. They often reply "peace of mind" or "a feeling of well-being" or "freedom from worry." At this point, they have identified a more fundamental want or desire. They have more clearly defined their inner world, or "picture album," which is crucial for effective counseling. This is accomplished more by questioning than by reflective techniques, statements of explanation, or the like. Of course, the latter methods can be useful when combined with or preceded by effective, skillful questioning.

2. To Gather Information

The gathering of information is not a final purpose of questioning. It is an intermediate purpose which aids the therapist in helping clients make value judgments and plan more effectively. Helping clients describe a specific day from morning until night can be immensely useful in providing cues for appropriate value-judgment questioning. If a depressing person says, "I got up at 11:00 A.M., ate some breakfast, watched TV in my bathrobe, took a nap, and looked out the window until 3:30 P.M.," the counselor has a wealth of information. Many questions can be asked which would help the client make value judgments. "Did your use of time work to your advantage?" "Did that kind of passivity really help you shake your depression?" "Does sleeping until 11:00 A.M. give you added energy?" Further information is gathered when questions are asked based on evaluation and planning procedures. If the client thinks it is helping to sleep until 11:00 A.M., it will be difficult, though not impossible, to make plans to change. Such information is helpful to a Reality Therapist.

3. To Give Information

A more subtle purpose for questioning is to give information. Paradoxically, this purpose is served best by de-emphasizing it as a purpose. For instance, in asking a client, "What do you want to do tonight to change your life for the better?," information is provided. There is an implicit message: "You have control over your life, and an immediate plan can help you take even better charge of your life." Similarly, if a client says, "I've been depressed for ten years. . . . It's so hard to get started in the morning," the counselor might say, "Will it really help you to keep looking back over the past and dredging it up again?"

Messages are more effectively communicated through questioning when the intent is not so much to inform or to deliver a message, but rather is to help clients focus their perceptions on their own behavior, evaluate it, and make plans. A further explanation of the paradoxical nature of Reality Therapy is explained in Chapter 7.

4. To Help Clients Take More Effective Control

Furthermore, mental and emotional strength is built only from the inside. It is not built by external stimuli. All motivation is *inner* motivation—that is, the fulfillment of wants and needs. Therefore, effective control of one's life, success identity, strength, and flexibility are attained from the inside. Questioning helps clients reach these qualities and aids them to define wants, to focus their perception on Doing behaviors, to evaluate them, and to make changes through effective planning. Statements, lectures, even force might satisfy those who are the statement-makers, lecturers, or the enforcers, but these methods fall on deaf ears; they fail to build inner strength and discipline unless the person is receptive. If force alone worked, there would be little re-occurrence of criminal behavior after a person leaves prison.

Still, the questioning used in Reality Therapy (see the cases cited in Chapter 9) is not a guarantee of results. In helping another person, the counselor, teacher, friend, or parent can only reach out. We all *choose* our behaviors. And so, skillful questioning, using Reality Therapy or any other method, is comparable to a lifeguard throwing a rope to a person fifty feet from shore. The lifeguard might be very skilled at rope throwing, perhaps was awarded a Ph.D. in rope throwing and the Olympic Gold Medal. Yet the person drowning still has the *choice* to grab the rope, to drown, or to attempt to swim without help. People choose most of their behaviors, and even the best assistance can be accepted or rejected.

Questions Frequently Asked About Reality Therapy

This is an attempt to answer questions most frequently asked about Reality Therapy. These questions have been taken from classes, workshops, and conversations about Reality Therapy.

Q: The Cycle of Counseling appears to be simple. Is it really as simple as it appears?

A: In developing the process and the theory, Glasser and others have intentionally used simple, down-to-earth language that most people can understand. It would not have been difficult to express these ideas in esoteric vocabulary which would be hard to understand. But such jargon would not help. One of the attractions of Reality Therapy as a counseling method or self-help tool is that it is understandable to most people. I regularly teach the method church groups, parents, and teacher assistants, as well as psychologists, social workers, nurses, counselors, teachers, and managers of every variety. They find the principles understandable and clear. Even a brief exposure to the process can provide an audience with practical, easily implemented ideas for dealing with clients, using with children, or applying to one's own life.

Yet the simplicity and practicality are a double-edge sword. It should not be concluded that Reality Therapy is a skill that is easy to master in all of its nuances. A brief explanation can provide some practical, usable ideas, yet to do the method thoroughly and consistently requires training and supervision. Reality Therapy is a method that is much easier to understand than it is to do. It requires skill, and any skill takes time and practice. The rules of a sport—for example, baseball—are easy to understand. Most fans have a knowledge of at least the rules and procedures of the game. Yet even the superstars don't play the game perfectly. In fact, the batting champion in the major leagues gets a hit fewer than half the times he is at bat.

In training groups to use the Cycle of Counseling, I have found that maintaining an integrated balance among the guidelines and procedures is difficult for the learner. After an initial exposure to the process, some parents report back with such statements as, "I grounded him, took away privileges, separated him from the family . . . really used consequences." Others say, "I tried to be friendly, asked her what she wanted and really wanted. But there's no change." It is easy to emphasize one aspect of Reality Therapy or one procedure to the exclusion of others. For example, the evaluation procedure is often omitted, even by trained counselors. It is easy to *understand* the importance of asking, "Is what you're doing helping?" *before* proceeding to a plan, but it is not as easy to remember to emphasize it in counseling a client or when a parent talks to a child. In a given moment, the helper's emotional behavior can diminish the clarity of the Thinking component, resulting in either a lack of integrated balance in use of the procedures or in the omission of a vital component such as evaluation.

In short, practicing Reality Therapy is a skill that can be continually improved through study, practice, and consultation.

Q: How does Reality Therapy differ from other methods of counseling?

A: This question is often asked in training sessions and workshops. In fact, it is the least important question in this chapter. Yet it should be discussed, at least in general.

Reality Therapy is similar to many modern counseling methods insofar as many of them are based on the assumption that human beings are in charge of their destinies and can change their lives. Existential counseling, Rational Emotive Therapy, and Adlerian counseling are based on this assumption. Reality Therapy is probably most similar to the Rational Emotive Therapy (RET) of Albert Ellis, yet there are significant differences. Reality Therapy accepts the human needs as "genetic instructions" that must be fulfilled. RET states that these are not human needs, that it is advantageous to have love, and so on, but it is not necessary. Rather, Rational Emotive Therapists believe that human disturbance is the result of irrational thinking, not of a failure to fulfill needs and wants. Consequently, in the practice of RET there is greater emphasis on the Thinking component than on the Doing component of the behavioral system.

Reality Therapy has been called a simplified version of operant conditioning. Yet in Reality Therapy, as currently practiced, the emphasis is not on the stimulus received from the outside world, but on inner needs, wants, and choices made by the client. It belongs more with the cognitive theories than with the behavioral theories.

Little space in this book is given to this question because of the impossibility of offering a complete and thorough explanation of all possible aspects of this relatively unimportant aspect. For a more thorough explanation, consult the many books on counseling theory. It is sufficient here to state that most prominent of differences between Reality Therapy and other counseling theories is the conceptualization of the process with the emphasis on evaluation: "Is what you are doing helping?" "Is what you want realistic?" "Does it help you to look at it that way?" "Are you going in the most desirable direction?" These are unique to Reality Therapy. Moreover, a detailed explanation of the unique theoretical background is explained by Glasser in his book *Control Theory* (1985).

Q: What is the place of feelings in Reality Therapy? Do Reality Therapists *deal* with feelings?

A: The answer to the first part of this question is, "They are *very important.*" To the second part of the question, the answer is an unequivocal "yes!" It is often erroneously stated that feelings are not important to the Reality Therapist, that they are not "dealt with" in Reality Therapy, that only superficial symptoms are discussed rather than root causes, and so on. Yet the opposite is true. Feelings are very important. As mentioned earlier in this book, they are similar to the warning lights on the dashboard of an automobile. When they are on, they indicate something is happening—that is, the car is functioning in a certain way. Thus a yellow light can mean that the cruise control is operating. Red lights often mean that the battery is low, the engine is overheating, and so on. Human feelings—positive or negative—are similar. They are very important to the functioning of the human system, just as physical pain indicates that there is something wrong and that medical attention is needed. More specifically, emotional upset—one of the negative symptoms—shows that there are unfulfilled needs and wants as well as that the person has made poor choices. For example, a person who feels depressed, or who more accurately is depressing, might be upset about the loss of a relationship. In this case the need for belonging is not met because the person retains a vivid, unfulfilled picture in a prominent place in the client's perceived world. The negative feelings of depressing are thus very important. They are the "red lights" that allow the person to seek help. Similarly, a person who wishes to keep a job or to obtain a promotion might experience ongoing irritation or fear. The pain of irritation or fear prompts that person to seek help in order to find a better way to drive his or her total behavior so that the want is fulfilled. And so the effective practitioner of Reality Therapy pays close attention to feelings, but does not separate them from total behavior because they are closely linked with Doing and Thinking.

167

And so in the process of exploring total behavior, it was stated earlier that there is emphasis on discussing the Doing component. Some people have erroneously concluded that feelings are not dealt with. Yet to talk endlessly about feelings is not really equivalent to "dealing" with them. In the behavioral system, there are Doing, Thinking, and Feeling components. To change the Doing component is to change the Feeling component, because behavior is total. Many people often feel tired in the morning. When the Doing aspect is changed, the Feeling component also changes. Behavior has many aspects. One component cannot be changed without changing all other components. Getting out of bed, exercising, clapping hands, singing in the shower, and dozens of other Doing behaviors help a person overcome drowsiness. Similarly, anyone who has driven for many hours knows the value of stopping the car, walking around a rest area, getting fresh air, and so on. Feelings of hunger and thirst are also "dealt with," not by talking about them but by changing the Doing component of the behavioral system—that is, by altering the most easily changed component of the behavioral system. The handle to the suitcase of total behaviors is attached to the Doing component.

The same can be said about feelings of resentment, guilt, anxiety, rejection, self-pity, worry, fear, and many others. When these feelings are generated, they are ultimately "dealt with" when the client can get beyond talking about them and can make positive Do-plans to change.

For instance, guilt about procrastination is dealt with by starting the task. Even if it is not completed, most people are astonished to find that merely beginning the task dissipates the guilt to a great extent. A workshop participant once told me that her grandmother gave her very wise advice, "When you're depressed, clean your oven." In terms of Reality Therapy she might have said, "when you choose a total behavior characterized by depressing, counteract it by choosing a total behavior characterized by a short-range, success-guaranteed Doing behavior."

Q: Can Reality Therapy be used with any client?

A: William Glasser, the founder of Reality Therapy, developed it at a mental hospital and a correctional institution. These are places where the "picture albums" and behavioral systems of the residents are very different from those of the majority of people. Such people are called "criminals," "deviants," "sociopaths," "schizophrenic," "psychotics," and so on. Reality Therapy was *first* applied to such individuals. It was subsequently applied to education, parenting, management, corrections, substance abuse, aging, and nearly every other setting in which one person interacts with another. People attending Glasser's seminars and my own Reality Therapy workshops represent nearly every walk of life. Some of the unexpected professions represented include lawyers, plastic surgeons, dentists, and physicians with a variety of specialities. I have conducted workshops for hospital staffs (for example, oncology departments), geriatric workers, Montessori school staffs, prison chaplins, pastoral care counselors, correctional officers, substance-abuse workers, managers and supervisors including foremen, state cabinet officials, presidents of companies, salespeople, first-line supervisors, and the like. It is a universally applicable method, and the application of it is limited only by the skill of the persons using it.

Q: If Reality Therapy is a helpful tool in counseling, does that mean that it can be used only when one person applies it to another person? Or could it be used as a self-help tool?

A: The Cycle of Counseling, as well as the principles underlying Reality Therapy described in Chapter 1, can be used as a very effective self-help tool. In fact, as Glasser frequently points out, this entire approach to helping people is more than a method or a technique. It is a way of life that must be utilized as a self-help tool by the professional person in his or her own life before it can be used effectively with others. If the helper's needs are not being met and if there is little knowledge and skill in how to meet them, there is little hope that such a person will be able to help another; "Nobody gives what he hasn't got." The person teaching auto safety should not be a high insurance risk.

169

Moreover, Reality Therapy and the underlying theory of brain functioning, Control Theory, should be taught to clients. They can learn to put it into practice—to examine what they need and want, what they are doing, whether it is working, and especially how to make plans to do better. They thus not only derive "insight" from counseling but learn to help themselves on their own.

Q: Isn't Reality Therapy merely a problem-solving technique?

A: No! As previously stated, Reality Therapy is based on a comprehensive theory of brain functioning. Therefore it encompasses all human behavior, and can thus be applied not only to specific problems, but to all human situations. It explains why a person laughs, cries, resents, depresses, becomes psychotic, and gets in trouble, as well as why someone is generous or desires to achieve a goal. It explains, for example, the profound truth in the age-old joke, "Why did the chicken cross the road? To get to the other side."

Moreover, Reality Therapy as a therapeutic tool is more than a superficial problem-solving technique. As Applegate says in the casebook *What Are You Doing?* (Glasser 1980), Reality Therapy is a strength-building tool; and as Glasser (1981, 1985) points out, its very purpose is to take more effective control of one's life. Incorporating the philosophy and the process of Reality Therapy often means making continuing and drastic changes in one's life. An isolated plan is sometimes necessary and is the beginning of control and strength (see Chapter 6). However, *repetitive* plans represent ongoing strength building and control of one's life. In my counseling, I help clients formulate a reading program of books which contain ideas similar to the principles of Reality Therapy. They subsequently report that they not only got new, practical ideas, but that they gained strength and now feel more self-confidence. This can be done with almost any client. To solve the problem of overweight, a person should eat less—a problem-solving technique of questionable value. But a program that includes reading, exercising, an assertiveness program, going to a group, and so forth, is more effective.

And so, problem solving is important in Reality Therapy. It is sometimes the beginning of a success identity, "strength," and more effective control. But the person with a "problem" needs to gain more basic strengths and more fundamental control before being able to solve problems.

Q: Are there any qualifications to practice Reality Therapy?

A: The answer to this question is a clear yes and no. There is a training program endorsed by the Institute for Reality Therapy. It requires attending workshops called "Intensive Weeks" and obtaining supervision from a qualified Reality Therapist. The details can be obtained by writing to the institute (address in Conclusion). This certification is an attempt to provide the public with practitioners who *genuinely* practice Reality Therapy, rather than a misinformed version of it.

On the other hand, even minimal exposure to the ideas can help a person be a more effective counselor, manager, parent, or friend. Learning not to criticize or to make or accept excuses; asking, "Is it helping?" rather than "Why?"; and making positive plans are ideas that can be learned and implemented in varying degrees. Even reading about Reality Therapy can be of immense value in learning to be a more effective person! At least this author is so convinced.

In conclusion, this chapter has reviewed some of the questions often raised about Reality Therapy. They are general questions about the principles of the theory and practice of Reality Theory. These answers are not final, but are intended to be discussed and rediscussed. If you have other questions, answers can be found elsewhere in this book or in the other books written on Reality Therapy (see Bibliography).

Postscript

This book has been written in easily understandable language, since Reality Therapy is, of its nature and by intention, designed to be usable. Those who have developed the principles and methods described in this book have explicitly shunned elitism and abstractness. Reality Therapy, therefore, is intended to be jargon-free, written in the everyday vocabulary used by the majority of people in the English-speaking world.

Yet this method is probably one of the most difficult to master. It appears easy, but this appearance is misleading. The way to learn Reality Therapy is by study and practice.

To meet this need there is a detailed training program in the use of these principles. It consists of learning the principles for use in a professional manner, and it is designed for counselors, therapists, teachers, nurses, psychologists, and professional helpers of all kinds. For more information, consult either of the following organizations:

Center for Reality Therapy
7777 Montgomery Road
Cincinnati, Ohio 45236
Tel: 513/561-1911

Institute for Reality Therapy
7301 Medical Center Drive
Canoga Park, Calif. 91307

Appendix:
Summary Description
of Reality Therapy

For those wishing a definition of Reality Therapy, the following description is provided:

Reality Therapy is a method of helping people take better control of their lives. It helps people identify and clarify what they want and need, and then evaluate whether they can realistically attain what they want. It helps them to examine their own behaviors and then evaluate them with clear criteria. This is followed by positive planning designed to help them control their own lives as well as fulfill their realistic wants and needs. The result is added strength, more self-confidence, better human relations, and a personal plan for a more effective life. It thus provides people with a self-help tool to use daily in coping with adversity, growing personally, and getting more effective control of their lives.

Reality Therapy is based on several principles:

1. People are responsible for their own behavior—not society, not heredity, not past history.
2. People can change and live more effective lives.
3. People behave for a purpose—to mold their environment as a sculptor molds clay, to match their own inner pictures of what they want.

The intended results described are achievable through continuous effort and hard work.

Bibliography

Alberti, R., and Emmons, M. *Your Perfect Right.* San Luis Obispo California: Impact, 1974.

Applegate, G. "If Only My Spouse Would Change." In *What Are You Doing?,* edited by N. Glasser. New York: Harper and Row, 1980.

———. *Techniques for Plan Making* (audiotapes). Los Angeles: Institute for Reality Therapy, 1979.

Blanchard, K. H., and Johnson, S. *One Minute Manager.* New York: William Morrow, 1982.

Callas, R., Pope, S., and Depauw, M. *Ethical Standards Casebook,* Falls Church, Va.: AACD, 1982.

Carkhuff, R., and Truax, C. *Toward Effective Counseling and Psychotherapy.* Chicago: Aldine, 1979.

Cornell, N. "Encouraging Responsibility." *Learning* 15, no. 2 (September 1986): 47–49.

Counselor and Social Worker Law. Revised Code, Ch. 4757. Columbus: State of Ohio, 1984.

Dreikurs, R. *Maintaining Sanity in the Classroom.* New York: Harper and Row, 1972.

Erickson, E. *Identity, Youth, and Crisis.* New York: Norton, 1968.

Fisher, L., et al. "Types of Paradoxical Intervention and Indication/Contraindication for Use in Clinical Practice." *Family Process* 20 (1981): 25–35.

Ford, E. *Permanent Love.* Minneapolis, Minnesota: Winston, 1981.

———. *Why Be Lonely?* Niles, Illinois: Argus, 1977.

Frankl, V. "Paradoxical Intention: A Logotherapeutic Technique." *American Journal of Psychotherapy* 14 (1960): 520–35.

———. *Man's Search For Meaning.* New York: Washington Square Press, 1963.

174

Bibliography

Glasser, N., ed. *What Are You Doing?* New York: Harper and Row, 1980.

Glasser, W. *Basic Concepts of Reality Therapy* (chart). Los Angeles: Institute for Reality Therapy, 1986.

_____. *Identity Society.* New York: Harper and Row, 1971.

_____. *Positive Addiction.* New York: Harper and Row, 1976.

_____. *Reality Therapy Tapes; Corrections.* Series 5, Tape I. Los Angeles: Institute for Reality Therapy, 1976.

_____. *Reality Therapy Tapes; Role Plays.* Series 3, Tape 7. Los Angeles: Institute for Reality Therapy, 1976.

_____. *Stations of the Mind.* New York: Harper and Row, 1981.

_____. *Control Theory.* New York: Harper & Row, 1985.

Glasser, W., and Karrass, C. *Both-Win Management.* New York: Harper and Row, 1980.

Hill, N. *The Master Key to Riches.* New York: Fawcett Crest, 1965.

Ivey, A. *Counseling and Psychotherapy.* Englewood Cliffs, N.J.: Prentice Hall, 1980.

Leefeldt, C., and Callenbach, E. *The Art of Friendship.* New York: Berkley, 1980.

Machlowitz, M. *Workaholics: Living With Them, Working With Them.* New York: NAL, 1981.

Maltz, M. *Psychocybernetics.* Englewood Cliffs, N.J.: Prentice-Hall, 1960.

Moore, T. V. *Personal Mental Hygiene.* New York: Grune and Stratton, 1944.

Peters, T., and Austin, N. *A Passion For Excellence.* New York: Warner Publishing, 1986.

_____, and Watterman, R. *In Search of Excellence.* New York: Harper and Row, 1982.

Powers, W. M. *Behavior, the Control of Perception.* Hawthorne, N.Y.: Aldine Press, 1973.

Sheehy, G. *Passages.* New York: E. P. Dutton, 1974.

Stone, W. C. *Success Through a Positive Mental Attitude.* New York: Pocket Books, 1977.

Straus, R. *Strategic Self Hypnosis.* Englewood Cliffs, N.J.: Prentice-Hall, 1982.

Weeks, G., and L'Abate, L. *Paradoxical Psychotherapy.* New York: Brunner/Mazel, 1982.

West, J., and Zarski, J. "The Counselor's Use of the Paradoxical Procedure in Family Therapy." *The Personnel and Guidance Journal* 62 (1983): 34–37.

Bibliography

Witmer, J. *Pathways to Personal Growth*. Muncie: Accelerated Development, 1985.

———. "Professional Disclosure in Licensure." *Counselor Education and Supervision* 18 (1978): 71–73.

Wrenn, G. *The World of the Contemporary Counselor*. Boston: Houghton Mifflin, 1973.

Wubbolding, R. "Balancing the Chart: 'Do It Person' and 'Positive Symptom Person.'" *Journal of Reality Therapy* 1 (1981): 4–7.

———, ed. *Dr. William Glasser on BCP Psychology* (audiotapes). Cincinnati: Convention Recorders, 1982.

———. *Changing Your Life for the Better*. Johnson City, Tenn.: Institute of Social Sciences and Arts, 1985.

———. "Reality Management: Getting Results" *Landmark* (Official Publication of Indo-American Society, Bombay) 11, no. 4 (April 1984): 6–8.

———. *Reality Therapy Training Intensive Workshop*. Cincinnati: Center for Reality Therapy, 1985.

Index

ABs ("always be"), 13–15
Acting out, 22, 125
Angering, 5, 6, 13, 26, 44, 46, 59, 68–71, 79, 85–86, 125, 133
Anxieting, 52, 85, 130
Applegate, G., 24, 40, 42, 62, 80, 103, 170
Arguments, avoiding, 15–16, 26, 100–1, 120
Assertive behaviors, 130–31
Attainable plans, 59–60, 65

Belonging (love), 1–2, 58, 62, 63, 111, 167
Bibliotherapy, 112–13

Choices, 5–6, 45–46, 83, 164
Commitment, 57, 154–55
  client, 29, 38, 55–56, 68, 71, 72
Communication, 11, 102–3, 106–7, 118–20, 162–63
Compromise, 100–1, 103, 120
Compulsing, 124, 125
Consequences, 19–20, 24–26, 143, 147, 155
Constructive actions, 130–32
Contributing behaviors, 130–31
Control, 20, 87, 99
  gaining, 46, 80–81, 126, 163–64
Control theory, 9, 81, 170
Counseling. *See also* Marriage counseling
  "do" vs. "talk," 37–38, 121
  family, 97–109

Counseling relationship, 10–27, 77, 103, 160, 164–65, 169
Criticism, 25–26, 80, 107, 143, 147, 155
Cycle of Counseling Using Reality Therapy, 77, 103, 160, 164–65, 169

Depressing, 5, 6, 42, 44, 51, 59, 62, 64–65, 79, 81, 83, 85, 110–11, 115, 125, 133, 162, 163, 167, 168
Determination, 13–14, 144
Doing Alone, 102–3, 117
Doing behavior (Acting; Action), 4–6, 39–50, 154, 163, 167–68
  client focus and, 42–43
  current emphasis on, 41–42
  description of, 40–41
  Feeling vs., 43–49, 52–53
  marriage counseling and, 92–94
  paradox and, 78–80
Doing Together Alone, 102–8, 117–18
Do-it behaviors, 122–24, 126–30
Do-plans, 45–46, 60, 168

Ethics, professional, 20–21, 57, 111
Evaluations (value judgments), 14, 29, 50–57, 63, 67–69, 111, 117
  perception and, 94–97
  planning and, 67–68
  Reality Performance Management and, 142, 145–46, 154

177

Index

Excuses, refusal to accept, 22–24, 143, 147, 155
Expectations of other people, 29, 34–35

Family counseling, 15, 97–109
Feelings, 4–6, 39, 167–68. *See also* Negative feelings; Positive feelings; *specific feelings*
  Doing vs., 43–49, 52–53
  marriage counseling and, 92
  paradox and, 78–79
Follow-through, Reality Performance Management and, 143, 146–47
Ford, E., 11, 60, 99
Frankl, Victor, 3, 84–85
Freedom, 2–3, 64–65, 111, 162
Friendship, 10–11, 17, 40, 75, 105–6
Frustrations, 4, 5, 29–32, 42
Fun, 2, 3, 62–63, 78, 82, 111, 145

Give-up behaviors, 122–24
Glasser, N., 40, 80, 170
Glasser, William, 1–3, 7, 10, 11, 13, 21, 25, 38, 40–42, 73–75, 77, 103, 107, 123, 142, 144, 146, 164, 167, 169, 170
Guilting, 5, 125, 133, 168

Hill, N., 112, 115
Humor, 16, 83, 135

Independence, 64–65, 116
Information, questioning and, 162–63
Institute for Reality Therapy, 171, 172

Karrass, C., 142, 144, 146
Kierkegaard, Sören, 63, 108

L'Abate, L., 83, 85, 88, 89
Leefeldt, C., 105–6

Maltz, M., 79–80, 112–13
Manicking, 110, 115
Marriage counseling, 42, 91–97
  case study of, 115–21
  doing and thinking and, 92–94
  intervention phase in, 100–8, 117–21
  perceptual systems and, 94–97
  wants and, 92–93, 116, 119

Mental Picture Album, 3, 21, 28–38, 99, 100, 110–11, 162, 169
  client's real wants and, 32–34
  client wants and, 28–32
  exploration of, 28–38
  "How do you look at it" question and, 36–37
  other people's expectations and, 29, 34–35
  paradoxical techniques and, 77–79
  planning and, 60, 61
Metaphors, 17–18

Needs, 23
  conflict in fulfillment of, 78
  fulfillment of, 77–78
  fundamental, 1–7, 9, 20–21. *See also* Belonging; Freedom; Fun; Power
  meeting of. *See* Mental Picture Album
  planning and, 58–59, 62–65
  Reality Performance Management and, 143, 151–52
Negative behavior, 5, 60, 62
Negative feelings, 5, 59, 167
Negative Symptom behaviors, 122–26
Negotiation, 101, 142, 146
Nervousing, 52, 75–76, 87, 113
Nonverbal communication, 11

Obsessing, 75, 115, 125

Paradoxical techniques (paradox), 69, 74–90, 163
  behavioral system and, 78–80
  case examples for, 89–90
  contraindications for use of, 88–89
  definition of, 74
  needs and, 77–78
  prescriptions, 82, 84–87
  process of Reality Therapy and, 80–82
  reasons for effectiveness of, 87–88
  reframing (relabeling or redefining), 82–84, 87
Perception, 6–7, 17, 21, 69–71, 163
  changes in, 81–82
  control of, 81
  evaluating, 54–55
  levels of, 13, 96

Index

Perception (*cont.*)
  marriage counseling and, 94–97
  Reality Performance Management
    and, 144, 153–54
Persistence, 26–27, 143, 148, 155–56
Phobicking, 85, 87
Physiologic behavior, 4, 5, 48
Planning (plans), 29, 46, 58–72, 163,
  165
  commitment to, 68, 71, 72
  completion of, 68–72
  Do-, 45–46, 60, 168
  doer-dependent, 60–61
  effectiveness of, 46, 56, 58–72
  evaluation of, 67–68
  failure of, 79
  immediate, 65
  marriage counseling and, 119–20
  need-fulfilling, 58–59, 62–65
  process-centered, 66–67
  realistic and attainable, 59–60, 65
  Reality Performance Management
    and, 154–55
  reinforcement of, 68
  repetitive, 62–65, 170
  simple, 59
  specific, 61–62
Positive behaviors, 5, 60, 62
Positive feelings, 5, 133–35, 167
Positive Symptom behaviors, 122–24,
  130–41
Positive thinking, 135–37
Power (achievement; self-worth;
  recognition), 2, 58, 63, 65, 78,
  110–11
Prescriptions, 82, 84–87
Problem-solving, 16, 64–65, 100–1,
  135, 170–71
Psychosing, 42, 125, 135
Psychosomatic symptoms and
  illnesses, 125–26, 137
Purposeful behavior, 1, 15, 78, 87

Questioning (questions), 61–62, 161–
  71
  about client wants, 28–34
  about other people's expectations,
    29, 34–35
  Doing behaviors and, 49
  Do-it behaviors and, 128–30

Questioning (*cont.*)
  frequently asked about Reality
    Therapy, 164–71
  "How do you look at it" question
    and, 36–37
  paradoxical techniques and, 82
  Positive Symptom behaviors and,
    131–40
  purposes of, 161–64
  "why," failure of, 22–24

Rational Emotive Therapy (RET), 166
Rational thinking, 135–37
Realistic plans, 59–60, 65
Reality Performance Management
  (RPM; Reality Management),
  142–60
  case examples of, 148–50, 156–60
  consequences and, 143, 147, 155
  follow-through and, 143, 146–47
  good relationships and, 142–45
  Job Examination Personal Profile
    (JEPP) and, 150–56
  laying it on the table and, 142, 145
  negotiations and, 142, 146
  no excuses and, 143, 147, 155
  persistence and, 143, 148, 155–56
  self-evaluation and, 142, 145–46
Reality Therapy. *See also specific*
  topics
  case studies of, 110–21
  conclusion for, 172
  information sources for, 172
  learning of, 77
  principles underlying, 3–7
  problem-solving vs., 64–65, 170–71
  process of, 80–82
  questions frequently asked about,
    164–71
  summary description of, 173
Reframing (relabeling or
  redefining), 82–84, 87
Relapses, 86–87
Repetitive plans, 62–65, 170
Replacement Program, 62, 122–41
Resenting, 59, 68–71, 79, 125, 133
Resistance, 59, 80, 86–87
Restraining a behavior, 85–86
Role-playing, 75–76, 150

Index

Self-evaluation, 142, 145–46
Self-pitying, 79, 85
Single woman, case study of, 110–15
Symptoms, 85

Thinking, 4–6, 39, 44, 48, 49, 50, 52,
   165, 167–68
   marriage counseling and, 92–94
   paradoxical techniques and, 77–79
   rational and positive, 135–37
Total behaviors, 20, 39–50, 81,
   167–68. *See also* Doing
   behavior; Feeling; Thinking
Trust, 11, 28, 62, 140

Unexpected, doing the, 15–16, 74–76,
   144

Walking, 63, 86, 108, 113, 118
Wants, 23, 69
   inner world of. *See* Mental Picture
   Album
   marriage counseling and, 92–93,
   116, 119
   realistic or attainable, 53–54
   Reality Performance Management
   and, 143, 152–53
Weeks, G., 83, 85, 88, 89
Wubbolding, Robert E., 75, 112, 118,
   142